Through the Pained-Glass Window of Twitter

The Trauma, Sorrow and Destruction of PARENTAL ALIENATION SYNDROME

Written by Marnie Grundman and Dan O'Shea

Edited by Jade A. Hernandez
Foreword by Bobbi Davis and Dawn O'Shea

B3D Enterprises LLC, Publisher

B3D ENTERPRISES LLC, Publisher

Through the Pained-Glass Window of Twitter

www.throughthepainedglass.com

First Edition

ISBN: 978-0-692-87227-7

Printed in the United States of America

The Apple of My Eye

It was May of 2009 and we were living in South Carolina. My daughter Megan had a swim meet in Jacksonville, Florida, where we stayed at a friend's vacation home in nearby St. Augustine. Their daughter, who babysat for Meg when she was younger, lived nearby and we took her to dinner and sat outside in the spring evening air listening to the live music.

While my wife and friend's daughter talked the entire night, my daughter and I did too. A night I'll never forget with her. We talked and laughed, and talked some more, with more laughter, the kind that comes from down deep, that says, "I don't want to be anywhere else, with anyone else, and simply your presence is the joy in my life."

Near the end of the evening a family that sat nearby was leaving and passed us on the way out. Walking at the very end of the group was an elderly woman, looking about 85 years old; she stopped where I was sitting and looked down at me and with a twinkle in her eyes she said, "I've been watching you two all night. She's the apple of your eye, isn't she?"

Taken by surprise, and once recovered, I shook my head yes in complete understanding, smiled at this kind and remarkable lady and answered as slowly as it was possible to say such short words, with a sigh from the core of my being, "Yes she is."

Love dripped off every word.

I don't believe I've ever had another conversation where so much was said, and so much was understood, in so little words, between two people who communicated for the briefest moment in time. Even now, I sometimes think an angel stopped and spoke to me.

Little did I know of the violent storm approaching . . . unseen, just beyond the distant horizon, swiftly and furiously heading my way.

Dedication

To Marnie Grundman. Without her help I could not have continued to "scratch the wounds" or endure the "PTSD flashbacks" while recalling the memories herein of great joys, great trauma and great sorrow, to put this in print.

To McSorley's on A1A and Mulligan's at Lauderdale-by-the-Sea. Mulligan's was my brief weekly oasis away from the alienation, a place to give my heart a break. McSorley's, who gave me the writing spot I needed, to look upon the sea, collect my thoughts, and write. It was also, after Megan was taken for the last time, where I began to meet Meg on a weekly basis - there, in the corner . . . *Through the Pained-Glass Window of Twitter.*

To Sandi, Maxie and Lulu. Without their friendship, my walk and path through alienation would have been much more difficult. I will always be grateful.

To My Sisters and Brother. They were there from the beginning of my life, at the beginning of my alienation, during my life, and during my alienation. I am deeply grateful having had them in my life. I could not have imagined my life without them and I am not sure I would have survived my journey without them.

To My Ex-Wife, the Mother of My Children. For the gifts of our children. Without her, we both could not have had the very special children we did. I will always treasure the wonderful memories I have had in my life, the times with her, and all of the amazing moments I shared with each of our four children.

To My Mom and Dad. They gave me a golden childhood, one of safety and security, and taught me the true values in this world – humility, respect, love, integrity and truth – what they gave me was eternal. Every day the void in my heart reflects their absence, the thoughts in my mind of them reflects their impact.

Lastly, and Most Important, to Each of My Four Children. Each so unique and gifted. I am proud of each one, who they became, and I will love them deeply, well beyond the day I die. They gave me the greatest joys and memories of my life, holding them, caring for them, crying with them, and laughing with them. I would not hand over one of these memories to remove the searing pain, torment and scars of alienation and estrangement. That is how powerful those memories are to me.

I am convinced that while peace has been elusive, eventually the love and memory of my children will be all that remains.

Table of Contents

Foreword i

Introduction iii

PART I BEGINNINGS

1 Mom & Dad 1

2 Through It All – My Sisters & Brother 5

3 Who's That Girl? – The Girl in the Orange Bikini 9

4 Our Children's Mother – Anne 15

5 For Just a Little While – Ryan, Colin and Erin 19

6 Come Play with Me – Moments with Meg, and Pooh 25

7 The Greatest Job in the World – Being Dad 33

PART II THE END OF THE BEGINNING

8 The Loss of Intimacy – The Beginning of the End 37

9 Five Desperate Minutes – Taking Everything I Ever Loved 63

10 Megan, Where Are You? – Memory Triggers and Ghosts 67

11 Goodbyes – Goodbye Meg, I Love You Very Much 97

12 All That Remains – Through the Pained-Glass Window of Twitter 131

PART III ALIENATION & ESTRANGEMENT

13 Parental Alienation Syndrome (PAS) 133

PART IV COURTS & COUNSELORS

14 Our Broken Judicial System – It Isn't Just About Our Children 153

15 The Psychiatric Community – Blinders on the Window of Alienation 167

PART V FINALITY

16 Letters to My Children 179

Epilogue 185

Reference 191

Through the Pained-Glass Window of Twitter

The Trauma, Sorrow and Destruction of
PARENTAL ALIENATION SYNDROME

Forward

It was always on her birthday, when the same question came to her mind when she woke up. "Will it be today?" she asked herself. And so, the little girl slid out of bed, dressed and started her journey down the long gravel driveway. Hope stirred, whispered to her, "Maybe this year . . . maybe this time." She arrived at the mailbox, reached up and opened it, and instead of the hoped-for happy birthday card from her daddy she only found emptiness again. She quietly closed the mailbox and headed back home, without the skip she had in her step heading towards the mailbox, and her pace slower than before. Her head bowed down as the tears welled in her eyes. "Maybe my Dad will send me one next year." The walk home was so much longer.

Or, of the little girl who asks - "Mommy, can I call Daddy today?" "Mommy, can I go see Daddy today?" "Mommy, did Daddy call yet?" Eventually the questions and anxious moments waiting for the phone to ring became less and less and the hope she held in her heart replaced with the hurt that burrowed itself deeper and deeper into her heart. The stars in her eyes slowly started to fade away and gradually the thoughts changed. "What is wrong with me?" "I'll be better next time." "Why doesn't he love me anymore?" "What did I do wrong?" The tall, good looking prince on a white horse who in her little-girl eyes could do no wrong . . . no longer saw her. He was gone. Maybe one day; maybe one day.

The little girl's Daddy woke up every day and asked his own questions: "What is my little girl doing now?" "How are her grades?" "Does she play sports, maybe Lacrosse like I used to?" "Does she have friends like she used to when I loved watching her play?" "Did she graduate from high school?" "Did she get a job and buy a car?" "Does she date?" "Did she marry and have children?" "Does she have someone she can ask for help and confide in when life hits, as he used to be able to ask and confide in his own Mom and Dad?" The father whose little girl was the apple of his eye knows she is growing and experiencing joys and sorrows that he is no longer a part of. The pretty little girl who stole her daddy's heart could no longer see him. She was gone. Maybe one day; maybe one day.

These are the actual words, thoughts, feelings, and emotions that an estranged or parental alienated child and a parent thinks, hopes, and feels every day. Parental Alienation is real and larger than life; it goes deeper than words can describe. For a child, it pierces the soul and changes the outlook of how they see themselves, an outlook that is then carried with them into adulthood. For the alienated parent, they live in a perpetual state of unknowns, wondering about the events and experiences of a child unseen. The choices we make in relationships, feelings of trustworthiness, our self-worth, that sense of constant betrayal and abandonment, it lies within our core. This is about the innocent children, the rights that must be protected in order to grow into responsible adults and parents. The time is now for the courts, lawyers, and medical professionals to come together - before it is too late.

People will never completely understand Parental Alienation Syndrome (PAS) unless it happens to them. It strikes without warning, turns your entire world upside down with grief and confusion, a void like no other. The loss of a child through PAS is felt by the entire family. In reality, it is FAS, Family Alienation Syndrome, not just PAS. The parent, the child, the entire extended family, their lives are forever changed, a piece forever missing from their lives.

This story is one man's journey through Parental Alienation Syndrome, into the unspeakable tragedy of losing all that he held dear. A man who never fathomed such a loss, a loving father and husband whose family was everything to him. A man, who through it all, never stopped loving. This man is our brother, and this is his story.

Dawn O'Shea & Bobbi Davis,
Dan O'Shea's Sisters

Introduction

I had no intention of writing a book on the subject of divorce, let alone Parental Alienation Syndrome. How could I? On our wedding day, I expected my marriage to be final. "Through better or for worse," as the saying goes, and as the priest stated on the day that I stood before God and married the love of my life. I did not take "if" with me to the altar. I didn't just marry my childhood sweetheart, I married my best friend. I married the only girl I ever dated, my first kiss, my one and only love.

Even as the marriage unraveled I believed we could find a way to come together. At a minimum, I believed that even as a divorced couple we would continue to co-parent our daughter, who was thirteen at the time, the youngest of four, the apple of my eye, my Meg. I never thought my wife, my best friend, the mother of my children, would ever want to take my children from me, or me from them.

I never imagined that my children would not be mine until my dying day. I was always their father, their supporter, their Daddy. I have always and will always love them with all my heart. To think that anyone could ever turn them against me, especially the woman who bore my children, the woman that I cannot ever remember not loving, would be the bearer to my loss and heartbreak in a completely indescribable way. I think that's why I never saw it coming, even as it was happening, I always thought that we would come out on the other side as our children's parents. I've come to learn that the perpetrators of Parental Alienation Syndrome rely on our blind trust to accomplish their goal.

After all is said and done, I am a father without children. My children are such without a father. We are all the victims of Parental Alienation Syndrome; as if our separation is not enough, we are not the only victims. All of our family relationships have been obliterated. Aunts and Uncles no longer exist as such. My children have lost their paternal extended family and all the beautiful times that would have been for almost the past decade. They have lost the future of those bonds that so many take for granted.

Parental Alienation Syndrome, or PAS, is not just about the parents and children. It's about the entire family unit. Everyone is fractured, everyone is ripped away except for the family that the alienator deems worthy. The rest of us die a slow agonizing death. Our titles and our identities are systematically stripped away.

My name is Dan O'Shea and this is my story. After over 30 years of being a husband, and the better part of my life as a father, my former wife and her family ripped apart the life I knew for my entire adult life over the course of a year. A plan that in retrospect was put into play long before I could have ever realized. I trusted my wife, she was after all, my everything. I cherished being her husband, and my place within our family. No one and nothing is perfect, but I truly had the life I felt I was meant to live, and I was grateful for my blessings. I looked forward to the days of grand-fatherhood and growing old with my wife.

I wish to be clear, that I am not sharing my story to unleash against my ex-wife. Even with all that has taken place, she is and will always be the love of my life and the mother of my children. I am sharing my story for future victims of PAS in the hopes that it will stop the progression through awareness. I am sharing my story to, in some small way if possible, to give comfort to alienated victims; *you are not alone.*

As a victim of Parental Alienation, I have learned that both fathers and mothers alienate their children from their spouse. PAS knows no gender, race, religion, stature in life or ethnicity. It holds no special favors to anyone, it lingers, stalks and attacks regardless of any background in life, and it attacks when its time and moment are ripe.

My story herein also, while speaking of our first three children, details more of our last child Megan. Not because I loved the first three less, but for several other reasons. First, I was given the privilege to enjoy daily moments with her when I left UPS and began my real estate career. Second, unlike our first three that could not have my undivided attention because they were close in age, her older siblings were moving on from childhood and away from their parents needed attention, Megan had our, my, undivided attention. Third, and most importantly, our first three came of age and their childhood lives spanned the time with both of their parents, like I did with mine, like their mother's childhood spanned with her parents.

Megan had no such opportunity, she was ripped from the love of two parents under one roof and of the natural course of having both of us there as she was moving on to high school, learning to drive, graduating, acquiring a first job and many other moments, occasions and events from childhood to young adulthood. Megan was 13 when the separation and the alienation began, so the subject matter of this book requires more attention to my experiences with her, describing through a father's eyes a loving childhood and the devastating holocaust of a childhood destroyed, simply because of a human action - the taking of a child.

For those having gone through all the traumatic stages of alienation, you understand already. I believe alienation and estrangement are extremely pervasive in our society, and we are a silent majority, silent simply because, (1) those who have not experienced alienation and all its symptoms cannot comprehend why it happened to the alienated, and (2) most courts and the psychiatric community for the most part have, extraordinarily, turned a blind eye - with intent. It has been discussed for almost a generation in those professions while families continue to be torn asunder in even greater numbers from Parental Alienation. For the victims of PAS - those parents and family members, there is no support.

I pray that my story, and my life experience, will shed light on a damaged system, and bring to light an issue that both courts and the American Psychiatric Association need to validate. We owe it to the children of divorce to protect their relationships with BOTH parents as well as their extended family. I also hope to de-stigmatize victims of PAS. When I chose to disclose that my children were taken from me (more accurately, that Megan was taken from me), I am almost always re-victimized. The mostly unspoken response is "he must have done something to lose his children." I am certain this is the case many times, just as I am certain that this is not the case many times. I have chosen to live in that place called "alone," rather than live in a world filled with judgment.

I hope my story, and the documents and experiences shared throughout this book, will shed light and alleviate the rush to judgment towards the alienated. I hope it will reduce the scourge of the leprosy of Parental Alienation placed upon them.

Why *Through the Pained-Glass Window of Twitter?* I wake up every day knowing that my children are experiencing joys and sorrows that I am no longer a part of. I wake up filled with thoughts of my children: What are they doing now? Do they have someone they can go to for help? Do they have someone they can safely confide in? Do they work, and what do they do? Did they move away from where I last knew, do they live elsewhere now?

I drift off to sleep with thoughts of my children: Did they fall in love? Did they get married? Did they bear a child and hold, hug and tickle their little girl or boy like I used to do with them?

Sometimes I find the answers through Twitter.

Every now and then I manage to find bits and pieces of my children. Glimpses of some of their life events play out on Twitter. I dare not "follow" them out of fear that my last window into their lives will be taken from me. I will not risk being "blocked" as their mother did to me with Megan's Facebook account at the beginning of my alienation.

It was through this pained-glass window of Twitter I found out that my eldest daughter Erin had married and was with child, eventually seeing my granddaughter for the first time. Periodically, randomly, I catch other beautiful life altering moments. In less than 140 characters (the maximum post allowed by Twitter) I have learned I was to be a grandfather for the second time. I learned of my son Colin's marriage, and that I am a grandfather a third-time over. Every now and again a photo will appear. Sadly, it's usually weeks or months between posts. My children's brief posts cause me to beam with pride and brim over with overwhelming sadness all in one breath.

I am my children's father, my grandchildren's grandfather, unbeknownst to them, I find bits and pieces of their lives "*Through the Pained-Glass Window of Twitter.*"

PART I - BEGINNINGS

Chapter 1

Mom & Dad

"The little toy dog is covered with dust,
But sturdy and stanch he stands."

After my Mom and Dad were gone, even all these years later, there is hardly a day that goes by that I don't think of them or miss them; I've come to realize they were imperfect parents, in an imperfect world, but to me, they were perfect.

I've thought often of all that they had done for me and the many happy times they had given me. I also thought of the periodic struggles, strife and difficulties they had, and how they worked through them.

Those two concepts above – that my parents weren't perfect, yet worked through their difficulties – made the beginning of my experience of Parental Alienation that much harder to grasp, or to even understand that something like it even existed. Instead of one of my parents pointing the blame at the other and wanting "out," they worked through difficulties as best they could, and even if they had not, they never would have ever thought of using one of us, my brother, sisters or me, as a tool for their vengeance.

Being a dad is what I did best. All I ever wanted in my life was to be a father. I wanted to be like my father, I wanted to be to my children who and what my father was to me. My Dad was 33 years old when I was born. He was always there for me, I grew up with the knowledge that I was always wanted and loved.

My Dad taught me how to treat my Mom with love, respect, and trust. He gave me a sense of security, and I knew he would always be there, through good times and bad. He taught me that life was not about material possessions. Our family was our wealth. Riches came in the form of humility, respect and honesty.

My father expected us to do well in school, anything less than a B was unacceptable. He watched our extracurricular activities and was proud of us, through success and failure. He was everything a dad should be and as I grew older, I realized I was blessed, especially when I saw so many other friends and neighbors who didn't have that. Simply put, my Dad was a powerful example of what a father should be.

Don O'Shea, that was my Dad. That's how they referred to him. From Baltimore to the Eastern Shore. He went to Polytech High School in Baltimore, Maryland, played for the Maryland Lacrosse Club, and was a lifeguard in Ocean City, Maryland. He was a man's man, tall and good looking with a killer smile. From what I've heard, the ladies loved him. Unfortunately for them, he had one love in his life: my Mom, Cecelia Mae Jenkins O'Shea.

My parents were very much in love. He always treated her the way a woman should be treated. He took great care of her always. They had their ups and downs like everyone does, but through their downs there was always a sense that everything would be ok. They worked through everything in life together, as partners in life should. They raised us with firm boundaries filled with love. When I disappointed my father, he would look at me in an audible way, through his eyes I could hear him saying, "You are so much better than that." That look alone would cause me to want to do better and to not disappoint him again.

My mother was not as silent as my father. She had a way of looking at you wherein her eyes would pierce your very soul. Her words, quietly spoken, would cut through me like a knife. Aware of this, she chose her words wisely. My mother used her words to impress upon me an appropriate fear mixed with common sense. She gave me words that I have lived by for my entire life, "Danny, no matter the cost, always do the right thing."

When I was 10 years old, living in Connecticut, I saw my Mom crying. Her mother, my Grandmother, Ella had died. She was the first person I ever knew personally who had died. For months afterwards, I would fall asleep in a tear-drenched pillow, exhausted from praying to someone or something to keep my parents from being taken away from me.

That was my awakening, when I first realized how powerful both Dad and Mom really were, and their presence. I couldn't imagine the void without him or her, either or both. The most important lives in my own life, they were far above all others, and they were equal in my eyes, my Mom and Dad. There wasn't a single moment in my life where I can recall that when one said something to me, it would not be confirmed by the other. My Mom's voice was my Dad's voice, and my Dad's voice was my Mom's voice, equal, shared and together.

Because of who my parents were and what they gave me, I wanted to be just like my Dad. I have fond memories of family road-trips with my parents. Many times, as we started a vacation my Mom would place linens on the floor in the back of the car to level out and take away the "tunnel" (a hump in the back seat on the floor of cars in the 1950's and 1960's). I would lay down in the "hole" for the trip – unforced, it's where I most wanted to be. It was from there that I could hear my Dad's voice as he spoke to my Mom. I would fall asleep to the buzz of my parent's quiet conversation. It was calm and sweet, there was a quality of love in and around their tone that gave me great security. I admired it, them and their relationship. I wanted to be them when I grew up. I wanted to give my children that same sense of love and security someday.

After my Mom died, many years after my Dad, our family gathered at the Cambridge Yacht club in a pre-gathering for her funeral. The Club sat on the Choptank River flowing in from the Chesapeake Bay and its condition spoke of a time gone by. I left the table as I thought of those times, and walked out onto the pier that overlooked the Choptank River and Route 50, both gateways to the ocean. From the west - Baltimore, where my Father was from and where I was first raised. To the east, the Eastern Shore and where my Mom grew up and Ocean City, all with countless memories.

My parents loved the life they shared, and they made sure that my sisters, brother and I did too. Get-togethers with family and friends, complete with Maryland steamed crabs for all. Trips to see extended family. Some of my fondest memories to this day are of the times we shared with grandparents, aunts, uncles, cousins, nieces and nephews. When we visited, it was times filled on their boat, in their pool, in their home, memories I will always treasure.

With such memories, I realized that with Parental Alienation, days, weeks, months and years of such wonderful times are forever taken away from a child alienated by a parent - not only from the other parent, but an entire side of one half of a family: grandmothers, grandfathers, aunts, uncles and cousins too. The tragedy is not only committed against the alienated parent, but most importantly, the child, who would never have the chance to make such memories to treasure. In my case, my children and my grandchildren forever separated from all current family members on his or her paternal side - and along with it a 300-year plus family legacy on the Eastern Shore.

Parental Alienation is not only an assault against a child and a parent by the other parent, it is an assault on a maternal or paternal side of the family too.

Chapter 2

Through It All –
My Sisters & Brother

"And the little toy soldier is red with rust,
And his musket moulds in his hands."

The most important people in my life are those I came to know shortly after my birth in January of 1959: my sister Pam, my sister Bobbi and my brother, Donnie, who were all here before me. A year after I was born, my best friend in life was born: my sister Dawn. This completed our family. Most of my memories are with my younger sister Dawn, as we were most alike and naturally did more things together.

One way or another while growing up, each of my siblings taught me valuable lessons in life, most times not even knowing it until long after. I remember waking up to loud pleadings one night when I was around ten years old. My Dad's voice was raised on the phone as he pled with his oldest daughter Pam to stay up, she lived several states away at the time, and had overdosed on pills. It was the first time I'd ever heard my Dad talk in such a tone, in anguish and fear for one of his children. Pam survived, but I don't think she ever knew what she herself gave me that night. I knew our Dad loved us, but to hear in such a horrific situation the sound of fear in the voice of a father, his incredible concern for the safety of his child, it only deepened my understanding of a father's love.

While Bobbi's time at home with us seems a passing memory, I know she took care of her younger brothers and sister. Instinctively, while the memory can't recall all of it, we know she had an impact on our lives. The many pictures of our youth remind us.

I can remember one day in particular I was returning home on the school bus. There were three bullies that rode the same bus. When we got off at our stop, they grabbed and threw my books on the ground. They started pushing and striking me, all three at once. Trying to defend myself I went after one, then the other, turn after turn while someone ran to get Bobbi. She came as all four of us were in tangles and broke us up. Needless to say, I was shaken. When we got home, Bobbi asked, and

I told her what happened. Instead of telling me I shouldn't fight, she gave me a lesson in fighting, in protecting myself. She put up her hands, told me to put up mine, and we boxed. Shortly, after all that happened, I lowered my hands and started crying. She hugged and comforted me.

I learned through Bobbi that we, as children, become an extension of our parents - both parents. Bobbi was the example set before us, she was a reflection of both of our parents.

From early in life until we started school, Dawn and I were always together. Of course, my brother Donnie was there much of the time as well, but my sister and I enjoyed more of the same things and activities. In summers on vacation, we shared the ocean, the beach and the two-seater bike our parent's friend let us use, riding it around our "second neighborhood." Coming home from high school, we had days of macaroni and cheese and hitting tennis balls on the street outside our home. I learned from Dawn that home was not where we lived, but really, where we were together, Mom, Dad, my sisters and brother.

Donnie was always my big brother. While just shy of a year apart in age, he always seemed older than that to me. I was the one who chatted, joked around and laughed all the time. He was the serious one and chose his words wisely. I always thought the way he spoke to me seemed to disrespect me. Over time I learned it wasn't that, it was that he took things so seriously he presented it as such.

I was 16 or so. My brother and I played Lacrosse, normally on the same team. When he moved on from our community Lacrosse team to high school the next year, I missed him. When he played varsity and I first played on the JV team, again I missed him. The void each season when we weren't on the same team was distinct. One particular day stands out for me; a friend and I had shown up near the end of a game that my brother had played in. He was hanging out with some of the other players after the game as "Lax" players do, drinking beer. I was a short distance from him when I saw the cigarette in his hand. He saw me. He approached, there was no judgment in my eyes and there was no "having to defend himself" in his eyes.

He told me, "Danny, don't ever start smoking, if you do, you won't be able to stop." That was it. He walked away and hung out, and I hung out for a bit. We never spoke of it again. I don't know if he even remembers. But he was my big brother and I listened and the simple fear, one of the greatest of human emotions, both good and bad, that fear of never being able to stop kept me from picking up the habit. His serious nature, his words of care and concern, prevented me from a life-long habit of addiction. Again, he was an extension of two parents who spoke as one.

My sisters and brother were there for me during my experience of Parental Alienation, these siblings of mine who I grew up with, who were a part of the life I treasured, my childhood. We fought at times, laughed at times, enjoyed each other's company at times, and many times they gave me words of advice out of their love for me. I never imagined that their words would take on the deepest of meanings for support, aid, survival and love at the beginning and during my alienation.

Chapter 3

Who's That Girl? –
The Girl in the Orange Bikini

"Time was when the little toy dog was new,
And the soldier was passing fair;"

I laid eyes on Anne for the first time at a prayer group church picnic in 1975, I was all of 16 years old. I will never forget the sight of her on the beach off the Chesapeake Bay. She was an absolute vision in a bright orange two-piece bathing suit. I watched her out of the corner of my eye while she splashed around in the water playing with some younger kids, which I later learned were her younger siblings. There wasn't a lot of interaction between us that day. All I could manage was to get close enough to her a couple times to make a comment here and there.

I had never been on a date before and had never kissed a girl. I was inexplicably drawn to her and I was attracted to her instantly. I wanted to connect with her, but being so young and completely inexperienced I had no idea how. As the day wore on I asked one of my friends in our church group if he knew anything about her. He replied, "You do know she's 20 years old, don't you?" Of course I didn't. I had no idea that she was 4 years older than me, she looked my age. Shocked, and disappointed, I thought, "Well, that's the end of that." I just knew that a 20-year old woman with a year of college under her belt was not going to be interested in a high school boy. I knew I could never compete with college men that would most certainly be vying for her attention. I forced myself to drop any further thought of her.

Not long after the beach day our youth group had a three-day weekend retreat at a house on the Severn River. I was fortunate that I had turned 16 a couple months prior to registration; I just made the minimum age requirement. I was also fortunate that Anne had not turned 21 yet, she was a month or two shy of being denied participation as a "youth member." That weekend was to be the catalyst for the beginning of a long, evolving friendship that would grow into the most beautiful kind of love.

When we all arrived, I noticed her, but I didn't allow myself to give her, or us, any thought. Why would I? The age difference was set in stone, and besides I was there to read, study scripture and to get to know others in the youth group . . . innocent me.

Not much time passed before we started making small talk. I wasn't one for talking, especially when it came to the opposite sex. Small talk was all I had to offer. It didn't help that she had her college roommate Sue with her. Being in the company of two older women highlighted that I was a high school kid all the more. My attraction to Anne was not anything less than it was the moment I first spotted her in her bright orange bikini. I simply accepted that to her I was just a kid.

On Saturday morning, some of the guys woke up with white faces, like badly made-up ghosts – myself included. Someone, or some *ones*, had conspired to put baby powder under our pillow cases. As we woke up, we didn't know we were each a victim until we began pointing at one another while roaring in laughter. We were gotten good, really good! I still laugh at that picture, and I miss those innocent times.

To add to the hilarious morning something even better happened that day. Every so often Anne and I would look over at each other and break out into a smile, for me that kind of shy grin that gives way to butterflies. What really knocked me over was her wink. I can still see it as clear as day. She started with a glance, then a smile followed by a wink. She had a remarkable way of doing it. At that point, I was an extremely wonderfully confused 16-year old with no idea how to respond. I just smiled back or made a little joke, while she and her girlfriend would lightly flirt back. Throughout the day, every so often, Anne would sneak a wink. It was now something between the two of us, our first "thing."

The following morning on Sunday, I was the sole beneficiary of waking up in baby powder. I had made my security check and double-check the night before. It was someone slick, experienced at using the powdery chemical. Stealthily slick. But why me? I didn't have any enemies I was aware of, certainly not within teenagers in a church youth group on a spiritual retreat. Not only did I question it, but a lot of the guys questioned it too. While relief for them, I was the focal point of "why him?"

The winks with Anne continued that final day of the retreat. But as these things normally do, questions raced through my mind. Is she really interested? What do I do? How do I do it? Restricted by age and the weekend coming to an end, I had no choice but to see her when I could, which meant prayer group events and youth group meetings. After all, I still had two years of high school left and college to go. Still my hope stirred, hope that I had a chance with her.

That afternoon, I had my longest "meet-up" with Anne, and Sue. As we chatted I thought aloud about the powder attack that morning, wondering what I had done, who had done it and why it was only done to me. Anne smiled and Sue began laughing uncontrollably . . . and Anne . . . Anne winked - a very long, slow wink. There was no admission of guilt, no more needed to be said, it was clear now. In that weekend of baby powder, innocent smiles and winks, there began a love affair between Anne and I that would last for the next 35 years.

Shortly after the retreat, one of my best friends and member of the youth group, Mike Decker and I were invited to Anne's home to spend the day at her community beach. As Anne and I sat in our beach chairs we began speaking beyond small talk. Our mutual attraction grew as we explored one another's interests. Lucky for us, our "romance" was helped along by Mike and another of my good friends, Kevin Mackin – and their driver's licenses. I still had a year to go before I could get mine.

Kevin, Mike and I lived in Crofton, Maryland, 20 minutes from Annapolis, and that summer of '75 was one to remember in the way that many kids have that "summer of." Mike and his sisters Debbie and Denise and their neighbor Liz and I would go to Annapolis every chance we could. We would meet up with other youth group friends to hang out and enjoy our carefree teenage time. For me, it was also my opportunity to keep seeing Anne.

It was during this period that Christian pop music was making its mark on the youth and the Jesus Movement was sweeping across America. Our youth group took hold of it and the likes of the 2nd Chapter of Acts, Love Song, Larry Norman, Phil Keaggy, Keith Green, Amy Grant and other artists played on our boom boxes more often than Fleetwood Mac, Genesis, Elton John, the Rolling Stones and other secular artists.

Starting in the early '70s, eleven festivals were held that summer from the west coast to the east coast of the United States. Our youth group planned to go to the Jesus '75 Music Festival in Lancaster, Pennsylvania. We packed up our cars, vans and trucks and made the trip with our camping gear from Annapolis to Lancaster. Anne and I conveniently sat together on the long trip in Mike's truck. It was at this time that I realized Anne lived in faded cut-off denim shorts, wearing them everywhere, and to this day they mark my summer of '75. Her legs were complemented by the jean shorts and the jean shorts equally complemented her legs. I don't know if it was easier to look at her or talk to her. I do know she looked as good, if not better, than in the orange bikini I first saw her in!

When we arrived at the festival grounds, it was like a Christian Woodstock. Youth everywhere, dressed in everything imaginable. It rained and poured, but spirits were high. Between the constant music and youth fellowship, none of us had ever experienced such an event. It was a Thursday to Sunday event, and we easily ignored the rain, heat and humidity. We were drenched in the sights, sounds and fun of being together and with thousands of other teens.

We wore bandanas around our necks and on our heads, soaked in water to keep us cool. We sat together, ate together and sang together. Even when the girls went off to do their thing and the guys did our thing, Anne and I always found time to be near one another.

The second night there, the torrential rain was so bad that we couldn't stay in the tents. Five or six of us girls and guys curled up in the back of Mike's truck for a night of shelter, and to hopefully catch up on the sleep we lost from the downpour the night before. Naturally, Anne and I made sure our sleeping bags were next to each other. While we all talked, each of our friends fell asleep. Everyone except Anne and me.

We laid on our sides facing each other, and as everyone else slept, we talked in whispers all through the night. Whenever someone tossed or turned, we went silent. Then, when all was quiet, we whispered again. We fell asleep in the early morning, at four or five in the morning. I don't know about Anne, but I knew at that point she was the girl I wanted to spend my life with, and while I was too young to think "the rest of my life," I knew I wanted to spend my existing life with her. There was no doubt it was a special night and something was "up," especially when some of our truck-mates commented the next day, "You two were talking all night!" Obviously, we didn't whisper quietly enough . . .

The festival not only cemented our close-knit youth group of friends, it also cemented a deeper relationship between Anne and me.

We made sure to keep close with more visits to her home and to the beach. Near the end of that remarkable summer of '75, four to five months after we met, Anne and I went with some of our friends to Ocean City, Maryland for the day, the beach resort 2 hours from Annapolis where I had spent many happy times with my Mom, Dad, sisters and brother. While the others went to the boardwalk to check out the game rooms, Anne and I hopped off the boardwalk to walk on the beach.

We stopped and sat together on a cement wall adjacent to the boardwalk, playfully flirting and talking. It wasn't planned, it was just inevitable. I was leaning close to her, my heart was racing, she had a nervous smile as I leaned over and kissed her. Not a long and deep kiss, but long enough. Long enough to know it was a natural evolution in our growing relationship. My heart was beating so hard I was sure that she could hear it. Several more times I leaned over and kissed her, wondering if I looked as nervous as she did. We talked and kissed a bit more, eventually standing up, knowing we'd better start walking back to the others. For the first time, we walked holding hands.

Those hands would be the hands that I would hold with my whole heart for the next thirty-five years.

Chapter 4

Our Children's Mother – Anne

"And that was the time when our Little Boy Blue,
Kissed them and put them there."

Anne and I blossomed together ever so quietly as the summer of '75 faded into fall. Our age difference could be construed as an "issue," as some of our youth group friends questioned how we could make a relationship work at that great of a gap. For Anne and me it really didn't matter at that point what anyone thought about our age difference. It didn't seem to be an issue to my parents and although I believe Anne's parents did have a bit of a discussion with her about it, it was not enough of an issue for them to stand in our way.

If there was ever a love-affair that started out as a friendship, this one was it. School started, my weekdays were spent in class and my nights were filled with homework, while Anne took the daily trip to D.C. to work. We didn't "make" time, we grabbed time. Whether it was on weekends together, the one night during the week at prayer meetings, or an irregular small church group dinner, we always found time to be with each other.

When weren't together, we spent hours on the phone. There were some nights I'd call her around 7 and the next thing I knew it was 9 or 10 p.m. The time just flew by. I don't know what it was about her voice, something about it kept me from hanging up the phone. My poor sister and brother would come in wanting to use the phone and I'd say I'm almost done. They would come back an hour later and yell at me and I'd tell them I'm getting off. Another half hour would pass and they would return. I'd tell them again, "I'm getting off, I'm getting off!" They'd come back fifteen minutes later on the "worst nights" screaming; Mom or Dad would come in and intervene, forcing a very unhappy me off the phone.

It was late October or November in 1975, our prayer group had a large dinner gathering at a member's home in Annapolis on a Friday or Saturday night. Anne and I "stole" some time alone sitting out in her car before she left later that night. She could drive and I couldn't yet. I was saying my goodbyes and we got caught up in some goodbye kisses. My younger cousin Joey had come out looking for me and when he came up to the window he saw us and our "goodbyes." He yelled, surprising us. He took off sprinting back inside. "Well," I said to Anne, "very shortly everyone is going to know now!" as it was not hard to envision him running inside screaming, "Danny and Anne are kissing in the car!" I don't know what Anne thought, but I just sat there and laughed. Of course, everyone knew before I even got out of the car. *Thanks Joey.*

Anne was the only girl I ever dated. Later, our friends jokingly said, "she robbed the cradle" and for the following year, because I didn't have my driver's license yet, she would come and pick me up on a Saturday or Sunday and drive us back to her house to spend time with her family. I didn't just love being with Anne, I loved being with her family. As time went on, even before we married, they became my family. We spent a great deal of time in their house, which sat upon a cliff overlooking the Severn River.

Anne had 6 younger brothers and sisters, Chris, Jean, Greg, Paul, David and Katie, aged in that order from oldest to youngest. Chris was amazing to me. He was the family "car repairman" and knew VW's through and through. At one point, a VW Rabbit, VW Bus, a VW Karmann Ghia, a VW Super Beetle and three VW Beetles sat in the driveway. Chris helped me purchase my first car, a VW Bug, and at times either helped or gave me advice on repairing my car. He was a fantastic son and brother. Jean and Greg were the two I related to the least simply because we had little in common. While Chris, Jean and Greg were mostly doing their thing being older teens, I became very close with Paul, David and Katie, the three youngest. They became my little brothers and sisters.

As in my own family, each child had their own different and unique personalities. Paul was the analytical one, it didn't surprise me when he chose a career in accounting, he had always been unique in my eyes. David was his opposite, he wore his emotions on his sleeves. As for Katie . . . looking back, she reminds me a lot of my youngest daughter Megan. A clear example of how different little girls are than boys, of how much smarter they are in how they think and relate to others.

Years later, when Katie married and had children, we were sitting out on my front porch and her father came up in our conversation and

I asked her, "Katie, do you remember your Dad?" She looked at me and paused, then said quietly, "No." I asked, "You don't remember what his voice sounds like, how he laughed?" Katie just shook her head no. My heart dipped with such a feeling of sadness. I didn't realize that feeling would later come a thousand-fold when my youngest daughter was taken by her mother without my knowledge. Katie was separated from her father by natural causes, while my daughter was separated from hers by an unnatural cause: the human hand.

When I was finally old enough to obtain my driver's license I was allowed to borrow one of the family cars, giving me even more time with Anne and her family. For most of 1976 and 1977 we spent the winters sledding and the summers going down to the community beach. We made Anne's parents' house into a personal sports stadium. The front yard was big enough to move our inside football game outside. Out back, a basketball court was put in, followed by a cement court. The hours spent in that backyard could not be counted. It was with them that I started my own annual "Holiday Lights" ride – packing the younger ones up in the car one night in December and driving through neighborhoods to see the very best homes lit up and decorated for Christmas. One day I wanted my own home to look like that, as my parents' home had, and to be able to drive my own children around for an annual holiday light show ride.

With the passing of time the relationship between Anne and I reached new and deeper levels. While our story reads in an idyllic sort of way it was not without its peaks and valleys. It was a relationship that was born from two people who shared the same values and understanding of commitment. Two people who knew that the peaks and valleys were the building blocks to a forever-lasting relationship.

By the end of 1978 it was pretty evident that Anne and I were very close and very serious in our relationship. She was working for her father, who was a CPA with his own business in Annapolis, and I was in my first year of attending Anne Arundel Community College. In early 1979, I was hired by United Parcel Service, Inc. as a part-time loader. At the time, I could not envision that it would become a 25-year career. One Saturday evening around that same time, Anne and I sat on the family room sofa for three hours before I finally gathered up enough courage to go upstairs and ask her parents if I could marry her.

With their blessing, it was decided that the wedding would be held on July 21, 1979 at St. Mary's Catholic Church in Annapolis, with the wedding reception to be held in her parent's backyard. Anne's parents decided it would be the perfect time to build steps from the house on the cliff to the private beach 100 or more feet below. That was part of their "backyard." At that time, the only way down or up was by a steep dirt path winding back and forth. As a family and family-to-be, Chris led the way and we pulled together and started plotting the foundation path, digging the post holes, adding the support beams, the steps, and finally the rails. It was months of work and months and months of bonding relationships that would go on until the end of Anne and me.

On the evening before our wedding it poured, all through the night into the early morning. It appeared the outdoor reception would be rained out as we were without any real backup plan. In the morning, the heavy rain turned to a light mist as the ceremony began. The service ended an hour and a half later, and as we walked out of the church, the light mist disappeared and the sun came out, glistening over the waters of the Severn River. The vision of the sun reflecting off the river appeared to be from heaven, and to me, a sure sign that we were a match made in heaven.

Boy meets girl, his first, his only love. Boy marries his one and only love. Boy has four beautiful children with his one and only love, and when their purpose was finished, together, the boy wanted to grow old with his one and only love. A fairy tale, story-book romance . . . it could have been.

It should have been.

Chapter 5

For Just a Little While – Ryan, Colin & Erin

"Now, don't you go till I come," he said,
"And don't you make any noise!"

Less than a year before marrying Anne, in the fall of 1978, I enrolled in the University of Maryland at College Park to earn a business degree. In the fall of 1980, I decided to forego the remaining time at college to work for UPS full time because Anne and I found out we were going to have our first child.

Anne and I were blessed with four beautiful, healthy children. As each one of my children were born, my greatest joy was holding them, watching them grow, learning to walk, learning to talk, taking in all those moments that occur between father and son, and father and daughter. I rejoiced with them, sharing their successes and supporting them through their failures.

I was twenty-two when my first son, Ryan, was born. Anne went into labor around 8:00 p.m. on March 19th, 1981. I had gone to pregnancy classes with Anne and during her labor, every 4-9 minutes, I breathed with her, held her hand, and supported her as best I could. Over thirty hours later, Ryan was born on the first day of spring, March 20, 1981 at 2:40 in the afternoon.

Ryan was born six months after I lost my father. I wept in joy and sorrow, as I was remembering my father's lifeless body, his spirit no longer present, and now I was witnessing a new soul in my baby boy. In six months, I had gone from being fatherless to being a father for the very first time.

As I wept, I can still recall a voice saying to me, "I am giving him to you for just a little while . . . and I will hold you accountable."

Those words held firm within my heart with each of my children.

I used to love taking Ryan to a nearby field to play. Sometimes I'd take my camera and snap tons of pictures of him. I wanted to make sure to keep those moments of him with me always. I knew how fast they were flying by. It's almost as if he went from baby to teen in the blink of an eye.

I will always remember one distinct event with Ryan that I would later relate to each one of my children. Ryan was between one and two years old, and he had just recently learned to walk. It was after dinner time and Anne had gone to run an errand. I was washing the dishes and Ryan was around the corner in the living room playing. Five to ten minutes into doing the dishes he came into the kitchen with a plastic bag over his head. I was stunned; I immediately rushed to grab it off his head. I will always remember the smile on his face after pulling the bag off, his quiet laugh over discovering something new, but as a parent my heart sank as he discovered something dangerous. I spanked him and immediately understood the maxim that "spanking a child hurts a parent more than the child."

Ryan didn't intentionally do anything wrong, but how could I sit him down and explain to him that he could suffocate and die, he did not yet know what death was, the sorrow a parent would endure for a lifetime. The pain of a spanking is all he would be able to relate to, not to do it again as I told him "no." I wept with him and afterwards sat with him and told him I loved him. He didn't understand the fear a parent has of losing a child, the fear I had of losing him. From then on, I understood the importance of spanking, but also the importance of doing so only to a child's bottom, where the sting is felt, but without injury, with only a hand, where a father could feel the sting too, so he would only go so far as love would tell him to.

With each of my children, discipline as such became the norm, words of love and encouragement and when spanking was warranted, only in the manner which started with Ryan. The discipline my wife and I gave, in agreement, was so effective that after each was two or three years old, they never had a physical spanking again.

Coincidently, Ryan went to the same high school as my Dad - Baltimore Polytech H.S. in Baltimore. I loved watching and cheering him on. In his senior year, early in the Lacrosse season, the team lost one of their best players. The coaches were hoping that as Captain, Ryan would pick up the loss. His first two or three games were disappointing and I could sense he was pressing. We had a long talk one night and I told him, "Ryan, you're pressing, you're worried about pleasing everyone else, just go out and be yourself, play for your enjoyment, be a threat to your opponent." His next game he scored three goals and as he approached the team bus, I walked up and told him, "That was the best game I ever saw you play." He smiled and said "Really?" He went on to be the player that the coaches had hoped for, scoring three goals in the Baltimore City Championship, the winning difference in the game.

Ryan was a great kid, with even greater values. I remember once while he was in high school there were a few days when Ryan wasn't himself. He was so quiet and subdued that I went to his room to see if he was okay. Tears welled up in his eyes as he shared with me what happened to affect his demeanor so. One of Ryan's best friends from childhood had driven him to a nearby neighborhood. His best friend began to stop and take mail out of mail boxes. Ryan told me he demanded his best friend drive him home. After he got home, his friend went back and not only continued to take mail, but also started lighting the mailboxes on fire. He was caught by the police and Ryan told me the police now wanted to talk to him. His "best friend" had told the police that Ryan helped him.

I told Ryan that he had tell the police everything. I called the officer in charge of the case and told him Ryan had nothing to hide and would answer all his questions. When the officer told me Ryan could be charged, I told the officer I don't think a judge would find Ryan a conspirator when he had demanded to be taken home as soon as his "best friend" started taking mail. I asked the officer, "Was Ryan in the car when you caught his friend?" The officer quietly said no.

I told Ryan to go to the station, tell them exactly what happened and if he was charged, we would deal with it. Ryan was truthful and hid nothing; he was never charged. I was so proud of him for standing up for himself.

I was twenty-three when my second child, Colin, was born. The labor was just as difficult for Anne as Ryan's, the only relief being that it was shorter. We worked together to bring him into the world, partners as always, and Anne again came through it strong. It was times like these I never questioned my partner in life was the right choice. Again, the quiet voice still spoke to me as it did with Ryan's birth, "I am giving him to you for just a little while . . . And I will hold you accountable." I was overjoyed at his birth, our second son.

I was ecstatic to have two sons to play and share experiences with!

Colin loved riding his big wheel out on the sidewalk. He'd ride it until the plastic wheels deteriorated; I can't count how many big wheels we went through. Colin was introspective. He was always quiet, but you knew his mind was taking everything in, like a little sponge. Unlike our other three children, Colin didn't seem like he studied or hit the books much, but he always had the best grades. The others had to work so hard at it, but for Colin, it was easy. When Colin's report card came out one semester in grade school, his grades had fallen. His mother showed me his report card when I had returned from a sweltering hot day of delivering packages for UPS.

I was hot, sticky, the salt from my body was apparent in the white stains on my brown shirt. I took Colin and Ryan (whose grades weren't that great either) for ice cream. I didn't even stop to shower. Before we hit Dairy Queen, I pulled the car over and stopped on the side of the rode. I quietly began to speak, while looking at Colin I said to them, "Is this what you'd like to do with your life? Look at me, I work from 8 in the morning until my truck is empty, working until 7, 8 or 9 at night. Never able to stop for myself or you, working for someone else. If this is what you want, then keep getting poor grades. If not, pick your grades up and you will have a chance to work for yourself and make better money. What you do now in school will follow you all the days of your life."

Colin's grades picked up (Ryan's too). Later, Colin joined the Army and completed his first enlistment as a communications specialist serving in Iraq. He went back into the Army and learned to fly Chinook helicopters, spending a second tour in Iraq and a number of years serving in Hawaii.

Both Ryan and Colin went on to serve their country in different careers. Ryan as a full-time firefighter in Charleston, SC, and Colin in the Army. I could not be prouder of them.

My third child was born four years after my sons on April 2, 1986. A much easier labor, it only lasted three or four hours. We were overjoyed as this was our first little girl. We named her Erin. I was lucky to have a little extra time with Erin as UPS gave us 3 days paid leave for childbirth. I relished the time home with my family and our new baby girl.

She was a very spirited girl from the outset; in the best way, Irish through and through. As she learned to walk, talk and be with her big brothers, I remember she never backed down. She was going to do everything they did. She had that determined look in all that she did. She wasn't "Daddy's Girl," she was too independent for that. She looked up to her big brothers and admired them, and as a Dad, I loved knowing that she had her big brothers to look after her.

Erin didn't involve herself as much in the "little girl things" many other little girls would, she was more of a tomboy, always trying to outdo her older brothers. It was a fun competition to witness, watching her wanting to do what they did, only better. There were many mornings as I was getting ready for work that I would see Ryan helping his brother and sister getting breakfast and lunches ready and Erin was right in the middle of it all.

I can recall one time when we were on vacation in Ocean City, Maryland, Erin was in the ocean with me; she was 7 or 8 years old and didn't yet have the courage to put her head under the water. I had my arms around her, pulling her up when the waves came. I told her, "When the wave comes, hold your nose tight, hold your breath and duck quickly." After a dozen times, I told her, "Now, I'm not going to hold onto you. I will be right next to you and have my hand on your back so you know I'm there." And so, Erin began to duck under the waves, knowing with my touch I was there should she struggle. Several dozen times Erin successfully lowered her head into the water. On one wave, I finally withdrew my hand just as she went under. She came up and quickly looked for me. I was there.

She smiled and I smiled back. I don't know who was prouder of her accomplishment, her or me. I remember thinking, this is what a dad does. Teaches, and supports. A dad is there, until it's time to let go.

And so it was with each of my children, Ryan, Colin, Erin and Megan.

Even though they're safe and living, even as they grew older at home, I miss when they were small, and all the dad-things involved. Before they even left for good, I periodically looked at pictures of them from years before. It was as if they had gone away forever, I wept even then, looking at them so small, seeing how they had grown.

When each left home, I wept every time. But I didn't want them to see me cry when they were leaving. They didn't understand it yet, and I knew it may take years to do so. They would have looked at me in puzzlement . . . a look of *oh please* or *geez*.

But they didn't understand . . . how could they?

They were excited! While I was in mourning.

For them . . . a new life was opening up! For me . . . a door was closing.

A parent's devotional duty inspired by the sincerest form of love was over - sacrifice.

The kind of sacrifice where a parent gave everything and asked for nothing in return.

Each time they left, my heart said I had to let them go . . . and at the same time that same heart wept as it said so.

Chapter 6

Come Play with Me – Moments with Meg, and Pooh

"So, toddling off to his trundle-bed,
He dreamt of the pretty toys;"

Megan, the last of our four children, was a surprise, coming into the world on June 20, 1996. Our boys were 14 and 15, and Erin was 10. I thought Anne and I were almost finished parenting and heading into the sunset as our boys were heading into high school with Erin right behind. I was not the least disappointed, but I was extremely concerned.

Anne was approaching forty, and a number of years earlier, Anne had miscarried. I was not only concerned about another miscarriage, but fearful for Anne as well. This pregnancy was different than our first three, because of the gravity I felt. Almost every night I gave Anne a body massage and I read to her and Meg (while in the womb) before we turned in for the night. Fortunately, Anne's pregnancy turned out extremely smooth and surprisingly uneventful.

After fifteen years working for UPS I had built-up sick days and vacation time. I took a week off along with the three days paid leave. On Meg's first night home Anne held her on her chest; I began reading to her as I had done during Anne's pregnancy so many times before. I will never forget how Meg, being a newborn and yet unable to see clearly, turned her head towards me. I could tell that she recognized my voice, and I felt so connected to her. In those early moments Megan became her "Daddy's Girl." No more important than my boys or Erin, and no less. The timing was different, and she was different, she was a girly-girl from the start.

Megan didn't have the luxury of her siblings being close in age to learn from and compete with. Megan had something different: she had her parents to herself. I felt a little extra blessed because Megan looked at me not only as her Dad, but as a built-in playmate as well. I would do the things she wanted to do. She often had my undivided attention.

When Meg was 3 and 4 years old, every summer during the work week I would get dressed for work and go downstairs and eat breakfast.

Some days, most days, she would get up and come down too. Megan would sit on my lap while I ate breakfast and watch me fix cereal. I would pour the cereal, pat it down, put in sugar and pour milk. Each morning the process was repeated.

It didn't take long before Megan caught on and it became a ritual. I'd sit down and I'd hear her little footsteps as she came down the steps, then she would climb onto my lap. I would pour the cereal, and she would pat it down. She'd pick up the sugar packs, I would open them and pour them on the cereal, along with the milk. I'd scoop a spoonful and give the first to her, then to me, back to her, then to me, until we were finished. I loved my mornings with Meg.

I'd come home from work many nights and she'd wait for me to play with her stuffed animals before she fell asleep, many times later after everyone else had eaten. Meg would have her "Princess" and "Elizabeth" and I'd have Hippo, and we'd have our "parties" and "nights out" until either it had been long enough or she started getting sleepy. Almost always before I took time to eat dinner. The nights she fell asleep before I left, I'd look upon her and quietly plead in a prayer to keep her safe.

In my reflective moments, I think down through my favorite moments over the years; whether money was tight or not, two things were constant - ice cream and Pooh. The hundreds of times stopping for ice cream with my children . . . all the laughter . . . priceless, forever cherished moments.

When Megan was 3 to 5 years old, she'd watch her *Winnie the Pooh* shows or movies. Many times I would sit or lay next to her. She would have her thumb in her mouth, giggling past her thumb as best she could. I long for the simplicity in those moments.

Those moments, my memories, they cannot be bought. There is no price. Just sitting and being. The presence of a daughter . . . the presence of a dad . . . combined it is a powerful force. One of the greatest powers on earth. I called those moments *Tasting Ice Cream* or *Sitting with Pooh.*

When Megan was four or five years old she used to love to ask me to play with her. On weekends, I'd be home working in my study on the computer or reading in bed. She would come walk in and come up to me and say, "Daddy, will you come and play with me?" She would ask with such a sweet little-girl inflection, with her beautiful blue eyes. Almost always I said okay, and we'd go play. In everything I've done in life, those moments were some of my happiest.

One day around that same time-period, Meg came in and asked me for help. She was "feeding" her dolls and wanted me to fill water in cups from the bathroom. As we were doing so, Mom yelled from the bedroom, not realizing I was with her, "Megan, you better not be getting water!" Meg had prior disasters with water and her dolls. When we finished filling, I said in a low voice, "You better not spill it, 'cause I'll get in trouble!" Looking up at me with a twinkle in her blue eyes and a precious smile with her lips closed, she shook her head in understanding . . . and melted my heart . . . again.

A year or so later, her Mom and I decided to give Meg her own room, as she had been sharing one with her older sister, Erin. The room we were giving her was my study. Ryan moved to South Carolina and Colin was going into the Army. I moved my office to the basement to make way. My desk, computer, printer and everything else. I redid the ceiling and walls, and refinished the floor. I redid the windows completely, sanding, painting the trim, replacing the glass. It would be Megan's room.

After a month of work, I was done and Meg's room was ready. We moved her bunkbed and the small desk I had used as a little boy into her new room. We put a small computer on the desk and I loaded up her favorite children's games. On moving-in day I came home from work and Anne said that when Megan was laying up top and her Mom was putting the sheets on the lower bunkbed, Meg had sighed with her head sitting in her hands and said, "I can't believe Daddy gave me his study!" I laughed and laughed.

Megan was becoming a "big" little girl. After several years it was time to set up her own email. I sat and pondered with her. "Megan, what would be a good email for you?" I asked, to myself and to her. Sitting on my lap, sitting on my leg with her chin in her hands, standing and leaning against me with her arm wrapped around me. We pondered as she changed to each of these positions. Pondering, every so often looking at her, into those beautiful blue eyes with the twinkle, like the sun reflecting off the deep blue ocean on a cloudless, blue-sky day. Then it came to me: I said, "Megs-of-Blue." MegsOfBlue. She smiled and shook her head yes. Her eyes are like the deep blue sky, her heart as big as the ocean; she used the email ever since.

For most of Megan's childhood she was a carefree little girl, she loved her friends and school, she loved life. She was a little social butterfly who never met a stranger. Megan was eight years old when my 25-year career with UPS ended. The loss of my job created the need to downsize and move. We took Megan from her neighborhood in Baltimore, her lifelong friends and a school she loved, and we moved to Seabrook, South Carolina on John's Island.

Unfortunately, Seabrook was an isolated community with no children her age, it was mostly retirees, snow-birds, vacationers and newlyweds; to make matters worse Megan's school was 45 minutes from our new home. She became a completely different child. She suffered from anxiety and stomach aches. During lunch and other breaks at school she would just sit at the lunch table crying with her head in her arms.

We took her to doctors for her stomach pains but they couldn't help her, the issues were psychological. We knew that we needed to make a change and get Megan what she needed, an environment that would give her the social outlets that we had left behind in Baltimore. We decided to move to Isle of Palms, South Carolina, just north of Charleston, a public, coastal community. We sent Megan to Sullivan's Island Elementary, one of the highest rated public schools in the nation that was closer to home, which was in a kid-friendly neighborhood.

I was working while Meg went to her first day at her new school. While driving home, I called Anne and asked her how Megan did at school. "Great! She was introduced to her new classmates and at recess, a number of girls came up and introduced themselves. Several who found out Megan was living nearby asked her if she wanted to go bike riding after school!" My heart was in my throat. Anne said, "They're probably over at the Rec center now," which was, so conveniently, in eye-sight of our new home.

I decided to go by it; there was Meg, in the distance, with two other new friends. I approached and rolled down my window as the three sat on their bikes on the corner. I said hello to Meg and her friends, and she introduced me to them. They smiled and said "hi" and I looked at Megan, wearing the biggest smile that spoke of her happiness in that moment. As I drove home a block away, I only had seconds to wipe the tears from my eyes, caused by the joy on Meg's face.

We enrolled her in the local summer league swim team and between that, her school, and our new neighborhood, Megan began making a slow but steady improvement. In the beginning of swimming, there were many tears, with the emotional and physical trauma caused by having to engage in a public activity. Anxiety or not she continued to make small steps as she swam in mostly exhibition events, still working up the courage to swim in any "ribbon" events. Her first big step was being invited by the swim team to compete in the Charleston city meet championships because some of the swimmers who had earned it were going away on vacation with their families. She swam one individual event, one relay event, and it was the beginning of her healing.

In the fall of 2006 Megan decided to try year-round swimming. After several months of practices three times a week, she had her first away meet. Dressed in her all-black Mount Pleasant Swim team suit, orange cap, and goggles, tears rolled off my eyes as Meg stood on the diving block that she was unable to do just several months before; behind her hung the University of South Carolina banners.

I normally took Megan to practices and stayed to watch. One day in late November I sat in my chair reading while she and the team swam. This practice, however, was different. There were no breaks. Lap after lap Meg and the swimmers continued freestyle, hitting the wall and returning. 15 minutes, 20 minutes, 30 minutes. At 35 minutes she appeared strained and her face was red and I could tell she was struggling a bit. I got up and went to Coach Steve and asked him what's going on as I had never seen a practice without breaks between different exercises. He smiled and said that it was a special practice, that the kids had to try to meet a certain amount of yards in a certain time. I asked him what she was attempting. He said 2400 yards in an hour. My jaw dropped. 24 football fields in an hour! I had to sit down, trying to let the distance sink in . . . while Meg continued to swim.

15 minutes to go. Megan's face was redder than normal and with each passing minute, her face appeared a bit more anguished. The last ten minutes I put my head down and prayed. Prayed that she succeeded. The minutes I'm sure passed too slowly for both of us. I couldn't bear to look. Finally, the hour was over. Megan was exhausted, but I had yet to learn the outcome. Not until I looked at Coach Steve and he smiled, Meg's tired face replaced with a beaming one.

Coach Steve went into the office while many girls grouped together, some celebrating their accomplishments. Out came Coach Steve handing a Certificate of Achievement to Meg, dated for that day, in honor of her accomplishing 2400 yards in an hour! I was bursting! The certificate was more than just a piece of paper. It was the mark of the last four months of her hard work, commitment, and the finality of overcoming her high anxiety. Watching, the tears flowed, Megan was going to be all right.

I was driving on "air" all the way home, telling Meg how proud I was of her. After dinner we gave her a wrist watch planned as a Christmas present. We took her to the Marble Slab, the local ice cream shop. I still joke that I am fortunate she wasn't sixteen at the time with her driver's license. I would have driven Meg to the nearest dealership and bought her a car! 2400 yards in an hour - 24 football fields!

Watching Megan swim with the rest of the team became a joy. I became the "unofficial team photographer" for the next year, just as I had years before for Ryan's lacrosse team. I didn't realize how powerful the images and videos I made of the swimmers that year were until the swim team banquet. The President of the swim team had one final award to give that night: "Our last award is to a volunteer parent who has done so much for our swimmers and kids, with the thousands of pictures we've been able to enjoy." At that moment, all eyes turned to me with shouts and cheering from all the swimmers; "Mr. O'Shea!" The swimmers yelled and applauded. I received a gift card from Starbucks, as they knew I loved to watch the swimmers practice with a cup of coffee.

The real reward was what I had found out while posting the swimmers image galleries and videos. The kids were able to send the links to parents, grandparents and family members who weren't able to see them swim – literally taking their hard work and accomplishments out beyond the four walls and the pool right to them. The other reward was especially satisfying – for shortly after that Megan stood alone in front of her entire school to give a speech. Then she danced alone in front of her entire school for a talent show. The anxiety-ridden little girl was gone and in her place was an accomplished girl who was clearly taking her place among her peers; Megan had overcome her high anxiety.

Within a year of being a part of the swim team Megan qualified to compete at the state level. By the time we moved to Florida in 2009, Megan was thriving. She had great close friends, a papillon puppy named

Sophie that she adored, and was excelling in swimming to a level that had a possible college scholarship written all over it.

Swimming aside, Megan was a normal teenage girl. She had a simple, innocent life that every little girl should have. Her Facebook was filled with friends and galleries of selfies of her and her friends that were more than pictures – they were creative art. At one point, a mother of one of Meg's swimming mates that we were sitting with at one of the swim meets said, "Periodically I look through Megan's image galleries, they are so fun to look at!"

Megan loved having and going to sleepovers, movies, shopping. Just the usual stuff that I didn't realize we took for granted because I believed we would be raising our daughter until she left home, just as we had with our older children. She was happy, funny and affectionate. Just a lovely girl growing into an even lovelier young woman. I could see, feel, a bright future for her. I was looking forward to her high school and college graduation. She would have been the first and only of my children to go to college and graduate. I dreamt of the day I would beam as I walked her down the aisle.

She was and always will be the apple of my eye.

Chapter 7

The Greatest Job in the World – Being Dad

"And, as he was dreaming, an angel song,
Awakened our Little Boy Blue."

Actually, the greatest job in the world is being Mom or being Dad. I titled this chapter "Being Dad" because it applied to me. The greatest thing about being a parent was "being there." It was through the years, before and after "being Dad," that I learned of the importance of "being there," and - after experiencing Parental Alienation - just how destructive to children the absence of "being there" truly is.

Shortly after my sons were born, Ryan and Colin, there was an event that occurred involving Paul, Anne's younger brother, that impacted me with respect to all of our children, that pushed me to make sure I could be there at any and all of my children's activities whenever I could. And while I couldn't be there all the time for Paul, David and Katie because of my full-time job with UPS, all of our spare time was spent with Anne's family.

Paul played baseball and I worked with him a lot, not that I knew a lot about the sport, but just to be there for him after his Dad passed away. I'll never forget his first baseball game that season. He was up at bat and had worked the count deep, I was hanging onto every pitch, just praying he'd get a hit. Finally, he lined the ball through the infield for a base hit. He landed on first and when he stopped, he turned to look over at me as I was standing behind the backstop. Our eyes met and he had the biggest grin. He couldn't see how ecstatic I was. Overjoyed for him! But at the same time the deep emotion of sadness swept in. His Dad didn't see it. He turned to prepare for a possible move to second place. I turned away so no one would see my tears. It showed me how valuable those moments are, how being there for what appears to be the little things are actually the largest and most important moments of all.

In the years leading up to my marriage and subsequent fatherhood, a popular song hit the airwaves called "Cats in the Cradle" by Harry Chapin; the main lyrics sung:

> "The cat's in the cradle and the silver spoon, little boy blue and the man in the moon. 'When you coming home, dad?' 'I don't know when, but we'll get together then.'"

When Ryan was just 3 years old, I was walking with him in the Annapolis Mall. He kept wanting to rush ahead. I finally decided to let him go. He was about 20-30 feet ahead of me and he finally realized I was not there. He began to look around for me, for my familiar face. I thought he would start to panic or cry, but he didn't. He just kept looking, for someone, for something. And it dawned on me, this is what happens with children who become fatherless or motherless. Eventually they're not quite sure what they're missing, but they know something is missing. They begin to search to replace what they are missing, the much-needed direction, but the path becomes harder and the path less clear; for some they find their replacement in the form of drugs, alcohol or who knows what else that may harm and impact their walk in life.

Time spent . . . being there . . . it's more than that, the moments, the very presence that the distance of Parental Alienation denies a child . . . whether it is enjoying a child's company, watching a performance, giving a helping hand or teaching a life lesson, these are moments that are "caught," unplanned. Yet it is these very moments that often stand out later as a child recounts their life, their parents - *if* Dad or Mom was there.

One night summed up the moments I had "being Dad" to my children: when Megan was fifteen and with me during my "shared time" when she took Sophie, her papillon dog, out for a walk. She came back into the house and didn't notice that she was tracking in dog feces from the bottom and side of one of her nice suede boots. I gave her a cleaner with bleach to clean off the feces. She went outside and came back in a minute later saying that she was afraid the cleaner would ruin her boot.

I pointed her in one direction while I moved in another, moving as one as we gathered the necessary materials to clean her boot. I had her fill a bottle from under the kitchen sink with water while I went to my bathroom and got cotton swabs. We went outside and, sitting together at the top of the apartment steps by our door, spent 15 minutes cleaning the ridges of her boot with the spray water and cotton swabs. Job well done, boot saved.

I was in my element, I was where I was meant to be, who I was meant to be. I was just being her Dad. Sitting next to her, helping her, meeting a need she had. This is what I had done a thousand times before, 30 years of "Being Dad" to my children. This is what I was best at. The little moments where I could get down with one of my kids and help them, enjoy them, and just be with them.

That's what I was thinking that night when I was sitting next to Meg.

Those moments became much less frequent when she was first taken to Texas by her mother. It was little things like those that the memory remembers, powerful moments of "being there."

With Parental Alienation, those are moments that are forever taken away.

In 1980, a year after Anne and I were married and before we had our first child Ryan, I will never forget the morning I answered the phone and couldn't hear my sister's words as she spoke in such anguish. I understood just one word: "Dad." I didn't hang up the phone, I just dropped it as I ran out to the car.

I lived just minutes from my parents' place, and as I raced my canary-yellow VW over to their home and turned into the long driveway, I saw the ambulance. I pulled the car onto the grass and jumped out, not realizing that I left the car running. My Dad was on his back in the driveway, the paramedics standing over him as I knelt down and put my hand on his leg.

Shortly after, I arrived at the hospital. I went into the emergency room and saw my Mom, my brother Donnie, and my sister Dawn sitting, waiting. Immediately my brother said to come with him. As we walked down the hallway, I asked him how Dad was. He wouldn't answer the question, even when I repeated it again - and again. Before we arrived at the private side entrance doors, I knew. I stopped asking, and instead started stating repeatedly, "Don't tell me." As we walked out the side double-doors, he simply said, "Dad is gone." He had died suddenly from a brain aneurysm.

I was crushed. I fell against the wall and just wailed. My Dad was gone.

I went back into the hospital wanting to see him, but he wasn't there.

That was my first instinct when I saw his body. The strength, gentleness and rock of a man I knew wasn't there. It didn't mean I couldn't say goodbye. "Thank you Dad," I whispered as I bent over and kissed his cheek, "For all you did. For always being there for me."

On September 23, 1980, the first day of fall, the season of death and dying, I was a son who became fatherless. Gone before his body touched the ground. I was 21 years old. My consolation? My anguished prayers all of those years ago as a boy were answered - he wasn't taken when I was young, he didn't leave me. He watched over me, took care of me and was always there.

As a child, I drenched my pillow in tears with those prayers, pleading that my parents would not be taken away. After Ryan was born, the tear-drenched pillow returned, but the prayers changed. Hoping my children's mother would not hear my pleas in the silence of the night, I prayed that I would not be taken away from my children, that they would know their Dad, that no harm would come to me that would leave them fatherless.

Many a night I kissed my little ones goodnight, laid down and wept in prayer. I prayed to the voice who spoke to me months and years before to let me finish the job of which I am held accountable for.

Never did I imagine that my job would be cut short, that my youngest would be taken from me. Never in my wildest dreams could I have foreseen our time together being cut short by Parental Alienation.

It was a late spring morning in 2001; I dreaded waking up. Ryan waited for me downstairs. I sat on the edge of the bed and I shook Anne, unable to speak. She awoke and asked me what was wrong, I could hardly get the words out, "Ryan's leaving …" And I wept.

It was a spring night in 2001, I was sitting in bed. Anne said to me, "Colin signed up for the Army, he will be leaving in the summer." And I wept.

In 2006 Erin made the decision that she wanted to go to Texas to live with her cousins. On the morning of her departure I hugged her goodbye, then I went into the house, sat at the table and laid my head in my hands . . . and I wept.

From March 20, 1981 until June 9, 2010 I had at least one child under my roof.

On June 9, 2010 . . . that all changed.

PART II – THE END OF THE BEGINNING

Chapter 8

The Loss of Intimacy – The Beginning of the End

"Oh! the years are many, the years are long,
But the little toy friends are true!"

From the moment Anne and I said "I do," I proudly took on the role of husband and provider. Over the course of fifteen years we had four beautiful children. Anne stayed home with our children and I went to work. I provided for my family as a UPS employee for most of our marriage. This was the life I was meant for.

I worked for UPS for the majority of our marriage, and in 2003, three years prior to an immediate twenty-five year-and-out earned retirement, I was fired for a policy that didn't exist, a practice that UPS and the Teamsters engaged in with a number of the older employees to save money on paying out the worker's compensation and full pensions, as the pension derived from the Teamsters Union.

After UPS, our life changed drastically. We sold our home where we lived for 18 years and I acquired my real estate license in Maryland, immediately transferring it when we moved to Seabrook on John's Island, South Carolina in 2004. While we had gone through big changes, we were going through them together, as a family, as it should have been. After a year in Seabrook we moved to Isle of Palms, SC and life began to stabilize fairly quickly.

Having to provide for the family over the years, I couldn't afford, both in time and money, to take the normal route of an education with college courses. I continued my education through online research, tutorials and study, focusing my efforts on web design and internet marketing. While doing so, I picked up part-time odd-jobs and continued building my real estate career, at one point working seven part-time jobs to keep us afloat.

I think it's then that I really realized what Anne did all day. From time to time Anne would teach an aerobics class for a little "pin" money, other than that she didn't contribute financially. She would take Megan to school, do morning prayers, then straighten the house. Once the house was in order she would spend the rest of the day reading the bible and other religious books, watching FOX news, and praying in bed. I would often return home to a bed filled with religious books. Books that Anne lived in, an imaginary perfect world that no one could touch or live up to, not even me.

This life she lived without me was a result of her upbringing, and of her mother becoming a nun after she was widowed. Even so, I never thought much about it. My family was not as devout. Maybe devout is the wrong word; we looked at religion differently. We lived by the golden rule, but did not judge those who did not. We lived our lives, made our own decisions. Anne would pray about getting a job rather than applying for one. When we had financial difficulties, Anne would tell me that I "was out of God's will" because I wasn't taking time before work for morning prayer.

When I worked for UPS I would make 160-180 deliveries per day, getting home between 7 p.m. and 10 p.m. from emptying out a truck that was full from top to bottom, front to back, exhausted from the day before. In the morning, the alarm would go off and I'd drag myself out of bed thinking of the horrible day ahead. Sometimes she'd actually tell me to make sure to get up after the first alarm ring so as not to wake her. There were many times that I tried to get up and have “prayer time,” but I was exhausted, physically and emotionally, and I just couldn't do it.

Throughout our time in South Carolina, I continued to support our family as Anne continued to take care of the home front. Never having placed a big value on money, we had what we needed, and that was all that mattered. Four years into my new career, which included starting a virtual tour internet company with my son Ryan, the real estate industry collapsed. Sadly, all of the part-time jobs did not come together enough to keep us from financial ruin. We declared bankruptcy in 2008.

In our final months in South Carolina, I was looking for and applying for jobs as an Internet Manager or Internet Director on the East Coast. I responded and interviewed for a position at a large car dealership in Orlando, Florida, at Carl Black of Orlando. Although Anne did not want to move she said that if I was hired for the position, our relocation to Florida would be an answer and she would comply with “God's will.”

Looking back, unbeknownst to me until the day Anne walked out, this marked the beginning of the end of our family, our marriage. Full time work was hard to find in the face of the real estate collapse and I had to take whatever I could find. Megan was now twelve years old, and our only child at home.

With the move and new job in Florida, I was required to work six days a week in rebuilding the dealership's internet department. Anne continued to stay at home, frustrated and bitter that I was never around. At a time when I desperately needed my wife, my partner in life, she was anything but. She became resentful of the time I spent working. She could have worked while Megan was at school. She could have built a life with me, as a supporter of our family, a life for herself outside of our home, a less lonely life. She chose not to and I accepted it. I never wavered from my role as the provider, husband and father. I suppose she also never wavered from the role she was born into. Wife, mother and devout catholic. Her life revolved around prayer and family, in that order.

The move gave us financial stability and a beautiful home in Oviedo, Florida. This return to a better quality of life should have strengthened our family. I was still working a lot, but I was able to be home evenings, and every other week I had two days off instead of one.

I would have stayed married to Anne until the end of time. Ups and downs or not, I loved her. Marriages experience unhappy times, commitment means you work through those times. For over thirty years we worked through those times. For thirty years I was a good husband, and father.

While I was a good husband, I was also a blind husband. Not because I didn't care. Because I was busy working and providing for our family. I was oblivious to the emails flying back and forth behind my back, undermining my marriage. I had no idea that my wife, my life partner, Anne was speaking poorly about me to her family and friends. Airing our disagreements to all who would listen, violating the sanctity of our relationship while playing the victim.

I grew up with parents who worked through disagreements. I grew up in a household where my father would serve my mother supper first, before himself and his children, in a demonstration of respect. The wife, the mother, comes first. I modeled that man, that life. My parents raised me to respect myself and others, to do the right thing at all costs. In the face of discord, no matter how heated, my father would have never thought to raise a hand to anyone, let alone my mother. He would walk away in the face of dispute. I, as a result, walked away from confrontations, waiting for cooler waters to drift in. Don't get me wrong, I wasn't perfect. There are things that I could have done better. Perfect or not I was committed to my family, my wife and the sanctity of our marriage, just like my father. When it came to my wife and my children, abandonment was not in my vocabulary.

While in many instances, the early signs of alienation of children by a parent cannot be seen, in most cases the early signs of a fractured marriage leading to divorce can. For me, it was approximately ten years into our marriage when Anne began confiding in her sister Jean about the supposed inner workings of our marriage. Together they decided that they were my psychologists, diagnosing my mental "conditions." For the next twenty years of our marriage, good husband, father and provider were at times exchanged for these "diagnoses," including that I:

1. Was obsessive-compulsive
2. Disliked women
3. Was an enabler
4. Couldn't hold a job
5. Was antisocial – didn't have friends
6. Was a narcissist

These labels flew whenever Anne and I had an argument, which wasn't often. Anne would tell me about these "labels," gathered by both she and Jean, as if that verified the allegations and made them fact.

After all of our years and all of my attempts to please my wife and support our family, even I had a limit. In that limit I put my foot down and defended my needs in a very big way for the first time in our marriage. Never would I have thought taking a stand would be the demise of the life I knew.

In 2009, after more than eight years of working 60 plus hours per week, struggling to not only keep our head above water but to stabilize us, we had begun to put a little money away for a family vacation in

August. In prior years, Anne and Megan had visited and taken a number of vacations with her family while I had stayed home and worked, so I was looking forward to not only a much needed break, but quality time with Anne and Megan, finally.

We could only afford a week, and we weren't going anywhere lavish, just an hour's drive away to Cocoa Beach. It could have been anywhere, it could have even been a staycation; I thought of little else but taking this trip with my family. The same could not be said for Anne and her family.

While I was looking forward to our long overdue vacation, unbeknownst to me Anne and her Mom were planning a vacation of their own. They were making plans to go to Barbados with Meg to visit David, Anne's brother – without me. The following were the actual emails between Anne and her Mom, not a word has been altered except those areas of privacy:

> 4/22/2010
> Mom, Phoebe the hummingbird is building a new nest in the rose bush. Wish you could see it. It's the cutest. Maybe a students computer could see it.
> Its www.-------.com
> Love,
> Anne
>
> PS got an email from David about offering to buy megan and me tickets to visit. We don't have updated passports and I just don't think we could do it At this time.
>
> --------------------
>
> From: Sr. Grace Sent: Friday, April 23, 2010 2:29 AM
> To: Anne
> Subject: Re:
>
> Anne, \i'm sad you can't go but \i do understand...\i'm sure there are several reasons...and \i want you to follow the leading of our \lord...nothing else

matters. \i will still try to get a ticket 19-24 to your place, if that's o.k. \i love you more than words can say.
you are beautiful mom

4/23/2010
Mom,
Have been praying about trip to davids. He said if we could get passports expedited ... he would get us tickets....i looked into it. Just not sure what we should do yet? It would cost $500 for both – renew for me, new for megan. I just don't know if I have it in me to get all the documents together. I spent most of the day just sitting with the Lord. I know david will need to know very soon. A part of me would just love to take the summer off of everything...but the practical responsible part of me says maybe not?? But its just for a short time? I'll just keep praying and trust the Lord to make it clearer in the days to come.

Listening for His song.......

Colin arrived at kates late Wed. night . I meant to email you yesterday but forgot in my anxiousness to 'skype' colin at kates. We finally got it 'skype' going but soon had to leave to take megan to practice and come home to start dinner, leave to get dan, then megan....etc...I'm wearing out. God will have to give me strength to continue...I offer it up to him. Anyway, colin is well. Had a week to relax. He'll have fun now he's with the family. We will try to skype later in the week. Its fine to come whenever...God plans it.

Love,
Anne

4/24/2010
Anne, you have to consider your own good health, spiritual, mental and physical. Maybe it would be good for you to take a break from responsibility. It's been two years since you were here...time for a break again!!! God will take care of Dan...He (God) is at work and He's not going to quit now. How much is there to getting all the papers together? Could you squeak out the 500---how come it's so much? I think they are only $100 (no more, maybe less) each. I can find out for you. I think all you have to do is get a picture at Walmart. (Get the cheapest and not too many...I think you would only need two or three max). I hope you thanked Dave for offering...it was his idea. I'll email him that you are reconsidering. It would do you so much good

Anne...you have to think about Megan too...she needs you and sometimes I wonder why you haven't had a breakdown before this...I know the answer...IT IS THE LORD. But He wants you to take care of yourself too. Selfishly I was looking forward to the possibility because I love being with you. And with Megan too. I'm happy Colin finally made it...I know they will all have a good time together. I'll be in touch. I love you
Mom

From: Sr. Grace

Sent: Saturday, April 24, 2010 3:27 PM
To: O'Shea, Anne
Subject: RE: colin at kates

Anne, I'm hoping you will seriously consider making this trip...it would be so good for you and charge your batteries for the future. You need to make a decision as I don't know how long the good ticket price will hold up. I will pray our Lord will help you decide soon...by tomorrow. I don't think it takes that long to get a passport...I will ask about that also. You could rest tomorrow and get started on that Monday. I think you go to the Post Office. I will be praying for you.
I love you,
Mom

4/24/2010
Mom, I am going to seriously consider going....i do think it would do me a lot of good. I don't know what to do with sophie....dans long hours and no one help out??? The passport expense is high because of quick turn around – I wouldn't want to plan it hoping they get here in time .... They are $100 each and $135 for expedited turn around.... I couldn't start the process till after May 5th . they say 4-6 weeks regular time. I'd be worried we might not get them in time. we had swim meet today getting up at 5:30 am...home at 2:30. Took a sort of nap for an hour an half.... Have to do it again tomorrow (Sunday). But we will have to go to evening church since we didn't do it tonight. Will have to drive dan to work and pick up this

week since we won't have money to fix his car until next weekend. God will have to help me but I won't make decision probably until Monday. Thank you for your prayers.
I love you,
Anne

From: Sr. Grace
Sent: Saturday, April 24, 2010 9:05 PM
To: O'Shea, Anne Subject:
RE: colin at kates

Anne, would you pay Donna back if I asked her to send you the money now? I would have to count on you to do it if I ask the favor of her. You have 8 weeks - I read on internet the main reason for delay is poor photos-they have to be two inches by two inches-the face full forward - head size one inch - and from the eyes down to bottom of picture l 1/8 - 1 3/8 inches. The K Mart in Steubenville is where we went (I was thinking it was walmart). Ask around where to get the pictures...you only need two it said on the U.S. State Department web site. And you do go in person to the US Post Office. Does Megan have one for when you went to Poland? It seems like if you have an old one to give in it may be quicker (seems reasonable). It's all done through the U.S. Post Office. Dan would take care of Sophi. She would be helpful company for him. Since he works so close he could come home for lunch.
They must give him time to eat!!!!!! I just know it can be done and you have got to have your "bucket filled" once in a

while as Sr. Katherine calls it!!! Let me know right away and I will ask Donna. I emailed Dave and he said he wants you to come...YES!!!!
I love you,
Mom

4/24/2010
Mom,
Yes, I can pay Donna back after May 5th. I will look into photos. Megan needs a new passport if she was under age whatever... we both will need new photos. I will look into what I can do about it. I do need my bucket filled.

And the more I've been thinking about it, I do think the Lord wants me to go, enjoy the rest, relaxation, & family. I would have had money to get things started but spent it on helping Katie with shoes for Natalia for first communion. Won't go into that now. Thank you for your help.
I love you,
Anne

From: Sr. Grace
Sent: Tuesday, April 27, 2010 8:59 AM
To: O'Shea, Anne
Subject: RE: colin at kates

Anne, I'm hoping that in spite of the move you can find yours, as well as Megan's, old passports. It is so much quicker if you've already had one and can present those. Isn't Donna a good sister???!!! love you and am excited about being with you and Megs.
Mom

Anne O'Shea" 04/27/10 3:02 PM
Yes, we have them. Xxx anne

The night of April 28, 2009 while Anne and I were lying in bed, she informed me that she was going to Barbados to visit David with her mother and Megan. I asked her how she was planning to pay for it, the only "extra" money we had was earmarked for our family getaway to Cocoa Beach. She told me she needed "a break," and that she was going to use the Cocoa Beach money for her and Megan to go to Barbados. I was hurt. I was furious. After words were exchanged I left our bedroom to take refuge in my study. I didn't want to continue arguing, I needed to think, I needed space.

As I made my way to the study just past Megan's room, Anne followed, yelling, and seemingly out of nowhere jumped on my back. Shocked, I asked her what she was doing as I attempted to remove her from my back. Meg had heard Anne yelling and I turned around to her guttural cry. I finally managed to pry Anne from my back and made my way to the study with Anne on my heels. I struggled with Anne, pushing her back as I closed the door. Once on the other side, I stood there shaking, trying to make sense of what had just happened.

The demise of our family vacation marked the beginning of our separation. I began to work from early morning until late at night, knowing Anne would be my judge and Jean, who had seen me a handful of times in twenty years, my jury. I knew, just like in the past that their communications would be flying back and forth. I didn't know how my life would be forever changed as a result of those emails. I didn't realize the beginning of our separation would forever rob me of my identity. My titles, Husband, Father . . . Dad . . . were about to be ripped away forever.

From: Sr. Grace
Sent: Sunday, May 02, 2010 2:36 PM
To: O'Shea, Anne
Subject: RE: Dearest Anne

Anne, are you thinking of not going to
Dave's. No pressure but he will need to

know soon. Can't Megan swim practice at Dave's? She wouldn't be missing much if she swims daily. Just like when you went to Dallas. I just know it would be good for you both...and it would be good for Dan. It is just our human nature to appreciate more when we don't have that which is so easily taken for granted. Please get the passports anyway...that is what Donna sent the money for. You can be deciding in the meantime. I will pray you will know God's will in this (I don't know what it is!).
I love you,
Mom

5/2/2010
Mom, I am planning on getting our passports. I know I will have to let David know very soon. Dan isn't taking this very well, and as a result Megan is saying she doesn't want to go and will stay and swim. I know that this isn't good for megan to feel this pressure from Dan. I am praying about how to handle it. I haven't heard anything specific from the Lord but I know Megan can practice swim at Davids. We will be missing a swim meet which in the big picture isn't important – its just that there are so few meets for long course which is what Dan is focusing on. I need Gods wisdom on how to handle this without it becoming a nightmare. I don't know if I should require Megan to come with me or I just come and let her make the choice to stay and Dan and she have to work out swim practice schedule. I don't know

what would be best at this time. I need
God to show me what is best for
everyone, His will. Thanks for your
prayers.
Love, Anne

5/2/2010
Alleluia!!! Yippeeeeee! You don't need to
consider extra charge for expediting...it's
so much faster when you turn in your
old one...I suppose you have looked up
U.S.State Department (then Passports).
I received a "sign" from our Lord in the
middle of the night that you will get
them on time....! I'm sooooo happy you
can go!!!!
love you tons, Mom

As Anne's Barbados holiday was coming together my heart was breaking apart. Our family vacation wasn't just fading, it was eclipsed. My soul hurt . . . my entire being hurt. I wanted, needed, a week with my wife and daughter. It had been over eight years since our last vacation. Eight years of working over 60 hours a week that was only going to allow us a week to enjoy one another unencumbered.

Anne held firm to her decision with dramatic flair. Instead of being truthful and telling her mother that the vacation fund we had was for the three of us to go to Cocoa Beach she told her mother that I "wanted Megan to stay home and swim." I only came to know this after seeing an email that Anne had left open on her computer. Never having ever looked at her email in our entire marriage, I was stunned when I began reading that Anne was telling her family it was only about Megan's swimming.

Several days later, after many late nights of hoping that the distance would allow our disagreement to settle down, I arrived home and approached the bedroom entrance hoping to have a calm discussion. Instead, I was met with a slew of accusations. Anne accused me of never supporting her. She told me that I was always working. She told me I preferred my mistresses - that's what she called my part-time jobs. At one point I asked her "if she'd rather I not have worked and we were on the street?" Her response, "Yes!" There was no logic in this discussion. The next thing I knew she was raising her arm and yelling, "Look what you did to me!" There on her arm was a large black and blue bruise, as if I had struck her.

On top of our discord, Anne was also talking with Megan day after day, asking her where she wanted to live, in Charleston, South Carolina or in Florida, away from me. My life, my marriage, and my daughter were being systematically manipulated away from me. I was being put on the defensive, backed into a corner, and I came out by playing right into Anne and Jean's calculating hands. Engulfed in anger, fear, and pain, I sent Anne the following (which is, like the emails prior - unedited):

> From: Dan
> Sent: Monday, May 03, 2010 1:13 PM
> To: Anne
> Subject: Issues Anne, Facts of our recent discussion that led to our most recent argument and what you told me
>
> 1. June trip with your mother:
>   1a - 'My' money was spent on expenses in the past year.'
>   1b - 'Because we don't have any money.'
> 2. Megan's swimming: 'I'm tired of being tied down.
> 3. Your new excuse for my anger, actions, whatever: 'Your job.' The above topics while different are the same underlying issues we've argued about in the past. The issues are always:
>
>   1 - Money,
>   2 - Our Children and,
>   3 - Your extreme inaccuracies of me which I am no longer going to tolerate.
>
> Issue One - Money
>
> If you don't want to use 'your' money,

get a job. I have 3 sisters who have a job and each of your sisters worked too. Don't tell me you had a job in June when for a period of time before that there was a break and even the June work came to an end. If it was a real job you wouldn't have had to use 'your' money. I regret I can't bring in $100k a year, no matter how hard I've tried.

Don't say to me periodically we'll 'trust the Lord' when you sit home, then when we're out of money, you've used all of 'your' money and then you complain and lash out at me because we don't have the money. I'd do a status check on your faith, because when the periodic 'financial trials' hit, your faith went out the door and you lash out at me. I know I've given my all and I don't need you to put me on a guilt trip.

Don't tell me I 'dragged you down here' after you specifically told me if the 'Lord provides a job, it is his will.' I remember that distinctly on a walk after spending months trying to find a job up in Charleston. I know one thing, I am not going to continue working 60 hours per week, hear not only do we not have any money, but your complaint of having to spend 'your' money.

Lastly, without money and if you spend (the money we don't have, in Barbados), how the hell do you expect we CAN have a vacation in August' My anger was justified. I reject your implication I have an anger problem. I have issue problems with you.

Issue Two - Our Children

Obviously we have different goals for

Megan. My goal is that if her gift in swimming could be converted to a college scholarship, she could have a great education our other three did not have. All I hear from you is 'she may not want to go to college.' So that's a reason to 'not' make her swimming a real commitment' Unless critical action is made now, either Virtual Tours takes off or you get a job (which I see neither happening at this point), or other, her future is not bright.

I see it, you don't, and assisting in her mind that she 'may not want to go to college', or she 'doesn't need to swim for half of June' only closes her options. It is unfortunate that your self-centeredness takes the form of 'I don't want to be tied down with swimming' when I fear Meg's future.

Further, this is not the first time one of our children ended up crying overhearing and being dramatically confronted with one of our arguments. I certainly am not going to remain in a heated argument OR remain in an argument where you want to point fingers at me that I reject. I am repulsed that I walked away to calm down and you chased me down as you recklessly do and did, and have our children overhear it, witness it and will forever remember it. To have Ryan, and now Megan observe your chasing me from our room, to the guest room and then to the study is abhorrent to me. To add, implying my 'anger' bruised your arm justifies my anger even more. YOU chased me, from room, to room to room. You aggressively would not physically leave me alone, continually trying to grab me.

I never hit you and my only response EVER was to keep you off me. If you decide to pursue this with legal authorities, I am only deeply and profoundly saddened you would force Megan to be a witness in this case. I am already deeply saddened that you have manipulated the bruising to the extreme that I 'abused' you. This is disgusting to me. I am also disgusted with what you most likely told your family. I know for a fact you've told them things about me that I would absolutely deny. This was highly evident when your Mother called 3-4 times one morning last month while I was at work and her tone of voice was almost like 'what did you do to her" At this point, I want nothing to do with your family. My anger was justified, I tried to walk away. I reject your implication that I have an anger problem. I have issue problems with you.

Issue Three After these serious arguments, you always find a new 'excuse'.

I can remember one of our first arguments you blamed me for 'not having any respect for women.' Still can't figure that one out. I can remember another accusation that I 'spent too much time on the computer.' This ultimately ended much of the association with Sue and Jared as I could see in their look 'why does he spend so much time on the computer' as if I was sitting in chat rooms. I was learning. Of course they never lost their job and thank god that after working 10 hours a day in a sweat box at UPS I'd come home and learn or god knows where I would have been to put food on the table for us.

This last accusation, it's my 'job' that causes my anger, no it's not. It's working 60+ hours a week, unable to put the time into Virtual Tours. I've worked for almost 30 years now with two companies that rely on intimidation by management and fear that you could be gone in an instant however manipulated and manufactured. So it's never been about 'disrespecting women', 'spending too much time on the computer', my 'job' or whatever new reason you want to give. You always point fingers at me and want me to be the blame. I reject them in the past and I reject them now.

I don't see anything redemptive for us now.

You are very unhappy and have been for quite a while. I have worked my butt off trying to give you and the kids a better life. Instead of getting a job and having money become an issue, we've had these horrible arguments and while continuing to do whatever I could to keep your distress down, the ultimate conclusion was you pointing fingers remarkably back at me. As long as enough money is coming in, having vacations with 'your' family, you're okay with me.

Being short of money, having to 'spend' your money, not being able to have a vacation with 'your' family and the accusations fly. Did you ever think that if you had a job and save money, I wouldn't have to have a job this demanding and we could enjoy vacations together instead of you and Megan flying off to Jean's or David's. Again, what money are you going to have in Barbados if we don't have any? Your excuse is you told your Mom we were still going on vacation, how the hell do we do that with money spent (we don't have in Barbados)' My anger is justified and I'm done with it.

In the past several years I began to believe more and more you no longer loved me. I sincerely believe that you don't now. I am convinced I was and am just a pay check for you - that you firmly believe you were 'dragged down here' (in your words) simply because it was where the pay check was. I don't believe you sincerely thought we'd have a vacation together in August. I don't know how you can concretely believe we'd have the money for you to spend in Barbados, vacation in August AND see Colin at Christmas. That is pure fantasy.

There's nothing left.

I expect to begin making preparations to leave. We have until the end of August to be finished. If you decide to stay, you will have to renew the lease, it won't be renewed in my name. Whatever you don't want, I'll have it put in storage or throw away. I strongly suggest you look into moving back to Charleston, SC. with Megan where the both of you want to go. Believe me, I've heard that enough times. However, as I said, I'm not going to work 6-7 jobs at the same time again.

If you decide to stay and refuse to make your own preparations, I'll make sure to have Shawn put the lease in your name. I will be gone September 1st, as August 1st is my goal to be out of Carl Black of Orlando. The retirement check will be yours.

I won't be living with Tom and Bobbi. I will find a room to rent, and work to hold me in an area I want to try to build up Virtual Tours and die trying to make it work.

This is non-negotiable. I'm not going to sit with you and continue to argue back and forth. At this point we are just going to agree to disagree. This has been ongoing for years and no longer. This will not continue. My daughter now has an image of us I can't imagine she'll live with for the rest of her life. It sickens me in the pit of my stomach. I know for a fact not one of our four children can say they EVER witnessed me hitting you.

1 - I certainly reject all of your accusations, 2 - you disagree with me, 3 ‘ we are not going to resolve these ‘years long’ issues, and 4 ‘ I am not going to continue in a situation where there are multiple false accusations targeted at me during an argument, resulting in horrible scenes in front of Megan while I'm the one trying to leave the situation, allegations of physical abuse, constant new ‘problems’ 'I' have and incredibly,

> being accused of having an 'anger' problem when that anger is completely justified AND controlled, even when you are chasing me down.
>
> Since it is apparent to you I am the one who has all the problems and apparent to me that this is nothing short of manufactured and manipulated by you, there is nothing left of value in this relationship.
>
> I've asked you for the financial information and am still waiting for it so this process can go as smoothly as possible.
>
> Dan

Anne responded the next day:

> 5/3/2010
>
> Dear Dan,
>
> Thank you for sending the email. My heart is broken seeing how my words and actions have hurt you and I'm sorry. Please forgive me. I see your perspective. I'm hurting too and need you to see my perspective. I say things sometimes without thinking it through. We need to learn to communicate in speaking and listening in love. I don't feel we are at a place we can communicate effectively without the help of a counselor. We are both feeling too wounded. Would you agree to work on our relationship with the help of a counselor? We are at this place because of decisions that both of us has made. I want to get help, please let me know if you want to. Yesterday, today, forever…I love you,

Anne

Unfortunately, Anne's response wasn't all it appeared to be. I would come to find out two short weeks later that she was just buying time.

We went to two counselors. The first we saw separately with the goal of later seeing the counselor together. I truly believed we were going to be able to repair our marriage. Anne was my wife, my partner, the love of my life. I never imagined that there was any bump we could not smooth out as long as we worked through it together. Imagine my surprise when the counselor informed me a second session together would not help. The second counselor gave me the same conclusion after we went for our individual sessions. To this day I have no idea what she told either of them.

When those counselors were gone, Anne then told me that "we needed counseling three times a week for at least several months." Counselors at that time billed at $120 to $150 per hour. I asked Anne "How are we going to afford over $1,400 in counseling bills per month?" Her response? "You figure it out." It was around this time that I began to notice how much time she and Jean were spending on the phone. As I went to pay the phone bill the number of minutes caught my eye. Upon closer inspection it became evident that they were speaking multiple times per day . . . or should I say plotting? In 15 days Anne went from "Yesterday, today, forever...I love you" to:

> 5/18/2010
>
> Dan, I had not made my decision as to what we were going to do. But after receiving your email this morning its clear we have different opinions and perspectives and it would be best for us to live separately, along with separate counseling. You have made it perfectly clear in your emails "I don't see anything redemptive for us now", "This isn't working", "There's nothing left", "This is non-negotiable", "Nothings left of value in this relationship".
> No point in arguing. We can make plans

> to remove our belongings from the house in the next month. You asked for the financial information. Please pay the bills.
>
> Anne

Two weeks after Anne's last email she informed my sister Dawn that she would be leaving our home. She refused to tell Dawn where she was going with my daughter. The communication between Anne and I was nonexistent.

After Meg saw her mother jump on me during that argument, I sought out counseling for her. Given the anxiety issues Megan had suffered years earlier, I was terrified that she would be damaged by the incident. On the days that I could not take Meg to counseling due to work, Anne was to do so. Anne not only skipped the appointments (which I would be billed for due to her not canceling), she did so without notice to me or the counselor. The counselor would later notify me that Megan hadn't shown up.

Prior to knowing that Anne was taking Megan and leaving, I made another "last ditch" effort to repair our marriage. I had found out I was eligible to receive my pension from the Teamsters Union/UPS and wanted to choose the right option that was best for both of us. I also wanted to try and save our marriage so I emailed Anne:

> From: Dan
> Sent: Friday, June 04, 2010 12:05 PM
> To: Anne
> Subject: Pension and Counseling
>
> My Dearest Anne,
> In the past day I have prayed about our pension and have decided I am going to hold off with the application.
>
> Based on the fact that you asked about "what happens if we do separate", and that this specific question is not going to be resolved soon, it is not prudent to rush into the pension. There are too many questions with respect to the

monthly benefit we will receive and what happens to portions of it if we indeed are separated or divorced that I could not agree with.

The only other alternative is to have an attorney oversee these issues and draw out an agreement.

I understand you do have other 'voices' you're speaking with and I don't believe they have my best interests in mind, all marriage privacy has been invaded and has been for years and with that all trust appears to be gone. Respect also.

I personally will always have a place in my heart for you and have not nor ever regretted your being given to me as a wife as a gift from the Lord. You have been and are a wonderful mother and gave me the gift of my children which there is no price for.

I would still like to go to counseling on Monday as a last ditch effort.

Of course we both have our deep issues with each other that at this point appear to be unresolvable. It is clear you have not forgiven me for years of things I am unaware of and it is hard for me now to understand your breach of our privacy as a married couple that has been ongoing for years.

Let me know if you are still wanting to go on Monday.

If not, and in the alternative, we should start making our plans to separate. In that separation I would also highly suggest divorce proceedings to get this concluded as quickly and least painfully as possible.

> This will allow you to petition the court for your half of the pension which in a joint option, would be approximately $750 per month. I will hold off on my portion of the pension.
>
> I would ask you to keep this as a private matter between us as a married couple, but know that is impossible as the private matters between a 'man and wife' in our relationship was first breached years ago and have been ever since.
>
> I will always love you.
> Dan

Five days later Meg was taken away for the first time. My time with Megan was going to be a battle. My best friend was to become my worst enemy, all in the name of saving face. God forbid a counselor hears the truth, and God forbid anyone other than her mother has access to Megan. Anne needed to paint me as the worst husband and father to ever walk the earth. I was demonized so that her sister Jean would support her both emotionally and financially.

Suddenly I was a complete stranger to Anne's family, whom I had known and loved since the age of sixteen.

Chapter 9

Five Desperate Minutes – Everything I Ever Loved

"Ay, faithful to Little Boy Blue they stand,
Each in the same old place –;"

From March 20, 1981 until June 9, 2010 I had at least one child under my roof. On June 9, 2010 that all changed. On June 7th, 2010 Anne told me she was leaving and taking Megan. When I asked where she was going, she replied, "You don't need to know where."

On the morning of Wednesday, June 9, 2010, the last day of the school year, I went into my study and waited . . . holding myself together until I heard the front door close. It was the finality of the sound that caused me to weep . . . until I heard a knock at the study door. Megan hadn't left. She wanted to say goodbye. I opened the door, with no time to wipe the tears from my cheeks. Megan said, "Goodbye Daddy." In a broken voice, I said, "Goodbye Megan, I love you very much." She walked out to the car and I looked on from the study window. I watched as the car backed out. The picture remains etched in my mind, Megan's mother staunchly looking ahead, accelerating forward, Megan wiping her cheek staring ahead in the passenger seat. And then nothing, but an empty driveway . . . and an even emptier house.

I wept when my children left home. When Megan left . . . I didn't weep; I sobbed. Not only sobbed; I wailed. For the first time in 29 years, 2 months, and 19 days, I was alone, without one of my children. And to end like this? 29 years, 2 months and 19 days of faithful commitment, to have my last child leave in this manner? Taken would be the appropriate word. And I knew not where Megan went.

That night marks the first night of my life where I didn't know where one of my children were when living under my roof. I had no idea where her mother had taken her, no idea where they would be living.

The following day, Thursday, June 10th, I called Megan's phone numerous times. No answer. I called her mother a number of times, again no answer. Finally, in the afternoon her mother answered one of my calls. "I've been trying to call Megan and want to speak with her."

Her mother replied, "You don't need to speak with her right now" and hung up.

The alienation had begun.

That evening I received an email from Megan's mother that I could pick Megan up from swim practice the next day, Friday afternoon, June 11th and spend some time with her. That Friday morning, June 11, 2010 I went to Megan's swim team practice to see Megan, only she wasn't there. I asked Megan's swim coach about her and he said that Megan told him her Aunt Jean was flying in to see her and she wouldn't be at practice.

I went to work and early in the evening left to go pick up Megan as I had done every week since she first started swimming in Florida. I gave Meg a big hug and asked her if she wanted to go eat something. Megan wanted to go home so off we went.

As Meg and I entered our home Anne and her sister were busy packing. I followed Megan to the living room where she laid on our sofa. The TV was on, but Meg wasn't watching it. She laid there staring at the wall to the left of it. The house was filled with the sounds of tape guns and possessions being put in boxes.

I asked Megan if she wanted to go somewhere, anywhere. I wanted to whisk her away from the sounds of "separation." She did not want to leave her home – I understood that, I understood she wanted to hold onto the last vestige of security that was being methodically packed away. I got up and walked out, crushed at what I was seeing.

I received a text from her mother 90-minutes later, "We're gone." I returned to find that half our marital property in the garage was removed, not just Anne's belongings, but our shared belongings, collected over thirty years of marriage.

My sister Bobbi and her husband Tom made the 90-minute drive from their home in Ocala, Florida the next morning. Marc, Bobbi's son, called to speak to me to offer his support. Bobbi was attempting to hand me the phone. I looked at her and shook my head, "Bobbi, I don't want to talk to anyone." Bobbi looked at me, putting her phone in my hand and said, "You need to talk to him." Marc was taken by his father when he was 12 years old and hidden for months before Bobbi found him and got him back legally. Knowing Marc had been through what Megan was enduring right now, the first thing that came to mind was a question; in a broken, defeated voice I asked, "Marc, what is Megan going through?"

Marc replied, "Guilt. She thinks it's all her fault." Marc said some other things as well, but I can't remember them. "Guilt" was all I held on to. My daughter was feeling guilt and responsibility for all that she was going through, exposed to. I sat on the sofa and wept.

Shortly after, as Bobbi, Tom and I went through the house to see what else had been taken, we were startled by Jean breaking in through a window. No doubt Anne told her I was working, as I usually did on Saturdays. They didn't take into account that this would be anything but a usual Saturday. Work was the last thing on my mind, the last thing I could cope with. Not thinking, just reacting, I called the police. Jean left before the police arrived and I filled them in on what was happening. They called both Megan's and Anne's phone until they reached Anne. After a short conversation, the police informed me that Anne would be there within 30 minutes to pick up the rest of her personal belongings.

Jean came marching in first, then Anne followed by Megan. I was stunned. Megan's eyes were teary, she did not look up and walked past the policemen to her room. Bobbi said while Anne and Jean were concerned about packing personal items, they left Megan in her room to fend for herself. Megan went from drawer to drawer, pacing place to place, touching things without picking them up or packing them and moving on to something else. She looked as if she was in shock.

Eventually the thought came to me and I asked the Sergeant, "Officer, can I go talk with Megan?" He replied, "Sure, she's your daughter."

Now I knew I only had a short time to get my words out before Megan would be gone again. What could I say that would help her and stay with her? I went into her room and asked, "Megan, can I talk to you?" She replied, "Yes." I took her into the guest room and closed the door. "Megan, where have you been staying?" She put her head down and replied, "I can't tell you." I asked her "Was it a home or an apartment?" "A home."

I asked Meg to sit down and I sat across from her, in front of her. Because of what Marc had said to me I found the following words: "Megan, this is not your fault." She looked at me and I wasn't sure she understood. "You did nothing wrong. This is a disagreement between your Mom and me."

I took her hand and held it in mine.

I repeated, "Megan, this is not your fault." And added, "They wanted to take things out of here that belonged to both Mom and I and they are not doing it in the right way, so I had to call the police. It will be done in the right manner and I will be seeing you soon and you will be staying with me too.

I repeated, for a third time, "Megan, this is not your fault."

I placed my hands on her cheeks, and I added, "You have been the most amazing little girl I have ever known. And you're growing up and you're still amazing me. You are an incredible person. I love you very much. Take care of your Mom, she is a wonderful mother."

I asked Megan for a hug. She stood up, put both arms around my neck, hugged me tight and kissed me on my cheek.

I was able to say what she needed to hear in those five desperate minutes. I could tell Megan's emotional state had changed, and so had mine. I was "settled" - more importantly, so was she.

After finishing packing some personal items Anne and Jean walked out. My little girl stopped and turned, the picture vivid. "Bye Daddy," she said. She came up and gave me the tightest hug . . . a kiss on the cheek . . . and then she was gone.

When my wife and her sister walked out of the house, the police Sergeant was walking behind them, and I was walking behind him. This was the same Sergeant who said I could talk to Megan, who my sister said sat in the house and looked upon the years of family pictures as he shook his head sadly. Suddenly, the Sergeant stopped; turning to look at me he said, "Treat it as if it was surgery." Immediately he turned away and walked on. I didn't realize immediately what he meant, nor did I in the days ahead, yet the words stuck with me.

Only later, after living through the pain and loss of Parental Alienation did I understand the sergeant's meaning. To react in retaliation, would lead to losing my daughter. He had seen enough to say those words to me, words that would guide me for years to come.

For two months I did not see Meg . . . and wondered if I would ever see her again.

Chapter 10

Megan, Where Are You? – Memory Triggers & Ghosts

"Awaiting the touch of a little hand,
The smile of a little face;"

Megan and I were to spend the day together on Sunday, June 13, 2010. My email, texts and calls the night before and that day went unanswered:

> From: Dan
> Sent: Sunday, June 13, 2010 8:59 AM
> To: Anne
> Subject: Megan on Sunday, June 13
> Anne,
>
> We agreed I could spend the day with Meg. I sent you a text message last night as to what time. You know I am home all day today. I just left a voicemail confirming 1 p.m.
>
> Megan on Friday night wanted me to take her to the pool.
>
> Dan

As I waited for a response, I kept myself busy organizing the items that Anne and Jean had not taken, especially in the garage. I put them into four piles: things I didn't want, things that belonged to Anne or me prior to our marriage, and lastly, things that belonged to both Anne and me.

The first thing I noticed was what was not there: family valuables, family pictures - and the Christmas ornaments. The ornaments were most noticeable, as they were the collection of almost thirty years of our family's Christmases. On the day after Thanksgiving every year, from the time my children were born, I took them to a Christmas Tree Farm. We would search for our special tree, find it, cut it down and return home to decorate it with our collected ornaments that we added to every year. The discovery of the missing ornaments left a pit in my stomach. The missing ornaments flew in the face of what Anne had been telling my sisters; all she said to them up to this point was, "I need to have a summer away."

The taking of our family heirlooms affirmed what my sister had said the morning prior when, after seeing what was missing, she gasped, "Oh my God Danny, they took everything you loved."

It would be another two days before I would hear anything from Anne. Two excruciating days of having no idea where my little girl was. I cannot tell you how many calls I made in that period or how many messages I left on both Anne and Meg's phones . . . pleading for a call or an email and finally an email from Megan, written by her mother:

> From: Megan
> Sent: Tuesday, June 15, 2010 7:23
> To: Dad
> Subject: fyi
>
> Dan,
>
> We're in Texas for a visit. Megan was talking with Erin and she thought it would be fun to see her sister for her birthday. Meg hopes to surprise Erin. You can reach me thru Meg's email. I cannot get into mine. Megan's phone has been acting up so it would be best to email her. You can also reach us on my cell phone. If I don't answer just leave me a message.
>
> Anne

The next email was made to look like my Meg wrote it. I knew it wasn't Megan. Meg *always* ended her emails to me with "megs."

> From: Megan To: Dan
> Sent: Jun 16, 2010 12:00
> Subject: hey dad!
>
> hey dad! !

i tried calling you but you didn't answer.
i will try again later.

love you!

love, megan

From: Dan
Date: Wed, June 16, 2010 12:05
To: Megan
Subject: Re: hey dad!

Megan,

There is no incoming record of your
call. Please try 3-4 times.

I love u.

Dan

From: Dan
Date: Wednesday, June 16, 2010 12 PM
To: Anne
Subject: Fw: hey dad!

Anne,

There was no incoming call that showed
Megan called.

Please let me speak with my daughter.

Less than a week after Megan was taken, not only was email non-existent, I had also been informed that Megan's phone was "acting up" and that her laptop had "broken" on the way to Texas.

From: Dan
Sent: Thursday, June 17, 2010 8:14 PM
To: Megan
Subject: Please Call

Hi Megs,

Please call me. I'll be up late, so you can

call me any time before you go to bed. I love and miss you.

Take care of your Mom.

Dad

At this point, I was calling Anne's and Jean's phones to speak with Meg. In the coming days and weeks when I would call Meg, not once was there an answer. And on the rare occasions when Anne allowed Meg to call me it was always under her watchful eyes - or should I say ears - and always when they were getting ready to head out the door, leaving us with only a few minutes to speak. My emails at night gave me small consolation:

From: Dan
Sent: June 19, 2010 10:49
To: Megan
Subject: Goodnight Megs

Goodnight Meg. I hope u had a great day. I love and miss u so much. Take care of your Mom.

Dad

June 20, 2010 was Megan's fourteenth birthday. I was unable to wish her a happy birthday, calling from morning throughout the day and into the night:

From: Dan
Sent: Sunday, June 20, 2010 10:09 AM
To: Anne; Megan
Subject: Megan's Voicemail

Megan, Please make sure Mom gets this. I'm sorry you had to be exposed to it.

Anne,

I tried calling Megan today on her cell phone to wish her happy birthday. Her voice mailbox is full. Please empty her voicemail or have her do it. If her phone is a problem and not working, I will buy her one and send it to her immediately. Let me know which option. You also want me to email directly to Megan's email, conversations such as these that Megan can be exposed to since your email is not working and you simply cannot open a new gmail account. You indicated I am to call you to get in touch with Megan. Please discontinue these alienation tactics and let me have normal communications as every father has with their child.

Dan

Megan...happy birthday,

I love and miss you so much.

Dad

From: Dan
June 20, 2010 9:30 PM
To: Megan
Subject: Cell Phone Meg,

Your voicemailbox is full. I guess you haven't been able to get my daily messages. I can get you a phone on ebay for the time being. Look for one and send me the link. I will get it and send it to you.

Tell your Mom I want to be able to call you too. When you get back we will go out and get a good one.

Dad

While I continued calling Megan to wish her a happy birthday, I shopped for two new cell phones. In one short conversation with Megan, I told her that I had bought a new phone for her and her mother. I was happy to send them, and Megan was of course, over-the-moon excited.

The excitement was short-lived as I received the following email:

> From: Anne 6/30/2010 4:39
> To: Dan
> Re: Ford & Phone
>
> You did not discuss this with me. I am shipping the phones back today. DO NOT ask Megan about the phones when u speak to her. U can always reach her on her current phone or Jean's home line.
>
> Anne

On July 1st I came home from work to find both cell phones had been "refused." The name of the person on the refusal was "Megan," written in her mother's handwriting. Megan never received her birthday present.

During this time Anne informed me that the two-week vacation was going to be a two-month vacation. I finally took my attorney's advice, filed for divorce and had her served. He told me that filing was the only way I would be able to get Megan back under Florida law. If I didn't, if Megan was in Texas longer than two months and started school there, it was unlikely that the court in Florida would bring her back.

In addition to filing for divorce I sent an email asking Anne if we could work things out. I asked her to come home so that we could attend counseling. Her response:

> Date: Fri, 2 Jul 2010 22:18:48 -0500
> From: Anne
> To: Dan
> Subject: Re: FW: email
> Dan,
>
> It's over. We are divorcing. It has been 30 years, 9 months, 1 week, and 46 days of opportunities, until you called the police and I was humiliated in my own home on June 12, 2010. You have emotionally and verbally abused me for

> almost our entire marriage. Receiving this letter, followed by your counter petition 19 hours later just confirms the cycle of abuse that I have endured. It is still all about you and what you want. You have violated every vow you said to me on our wedding day.
>
> Megan said you asked her if I had discussed us returning. She and I have discussed everything including relocation. She was afraid to tell you.
>
> You have made it perfectly clear, quoting from your emails, "I don't see anything redemptive for us now", "This isn't working", "There is nothing left", "This is non-negotiable", "Nothings left of value in this relationship".
> Agreed. It's over.
>
> Anne

On July 4, 2010, my emotional and physiological reactions to Anne alienating me from Meg erupted in full force. I visited my sister Bobbi and her husband Tom in Ocala. During my career with UPS I had always gotten this holiday off, and I had always spent it with our children, enjoying family picnics and fireworks. Bobbi and Tom were going to visit his mother for a Fourth of July brunch at her assisted living residence with her and a number of her friends. Periodically the sorrow hit as I couldn't stop thinking of Meg. Each time tears welled in my eyes I excused myself and went to the empty community office nearby; there I sat alone, sobbing uncontrollably. After the third or fourth time excusing myself, Bobbi came in and sat next to me, knowing why I left each time. She sat with me, her hand on mine, consoling me.

Late on many nights, after numerous attempts to call Megan, I'd call just to hear her voice on her "broken" phone's voicemail; eventually Anne took that away too . . . by removing her voice.

And the visions began:

> I'd see Meg in our family room doing her homework …
>
> I'd look out in the backyard and there she stood with her little papillon puppy, Sophie . . .
>
> I'd walk into the kitchen and she'd look up at me from the table with her beautiful smile . . .
>
> I'd drive by the pool where she was a Junior Olympic swimmer; upon seeing me, she would head my way . . .
>
> But each time I saw her, her ghost would fade away.
>
> I used to think the term "broken heart" was a figure of speech, fine prose for a writer's fictional story.
>
> Until I experienced the reality of a broken heart firsthand.
>
> Each time Megan faded away, my heart heaved, shuddered, and wept, uncontrolled by number, time or place.
>
> I drove by places that once were joyful memories turned into daily reminders of a painful loss. Memory triggers and burns.
>
> Reminders of what was . . . what now is.
>
> Daily, nightly, an uninvited guest appeared - fear, whispering to me, "*You'll never see her again.*"
>
> Deep sadness became a companion who walked beside me in those two months.

As the first month of Megan's alienation and abduction approached, I discovered that not only was I being alienated (along with my family), but Megan's friends in Florida were too. Despite being removed as one of Megan's "friends" on Facebook, I was able to see recent posts on her page. One night I went to her page to see that her best friend at the time, Lizzie, had posted - "*Megan, where are you? I miss you a little . . . well, a lot.*"

Even Meg's own girlfriends were being alienated.

Heading into the summer of 2010, I thought Megan was going to have one of the best summers ever. Knowing Meg, I could see it. She would have morning swim practice in the Florida sun and time with her swimming friends. Then home for a mid-morning nap. Afterwards time spent with all of her non-swimming friends, sleep overs, shopping at the mall, movies, and more. It was all a father wanted, to watch his daughter grow and enjoy the summer as her first year of high school approached. All gone. Taken away. Not from me – from her.

In one of my next short conversations with Megan I asked her if there were any girls in the neighborhood there. Meg told me there was a girl down the street; I asked her if she had made friends with her. Megan said "no" and when I asked her why, she responded, "I don't want to."

At one point, I asked Meg what she did with her time. She said, "Well, I clean for Jean and Jamie and earn some money so I have some when I go shopping." I asked her what she cleaned and she said she cleaned rooms and did some of the laundry. Imagine, this was to be the "Summer of Megan" - my daughter had instead become the servant of Jamie Reed, Head Trainer of the Texas Rangers, and his wife Jean.

Heading into the second month Megan was taken, things changed for the better because of the pending legal action. Communication improved a bit with Megan and me, and I also found out that Megan was able to begin communicating with her friends in Florida. It was clear that there would be a pending return of Megan to Florida and that if she was not returned by August 13, 2010, my wife could be held in contempt for child abduction and returned under court order.

In early July I was emailing and calling Colin, my second son; I hadn't heard from him for almost a week. When I did finally hear from him his reply was startling and heartbreaking:

> From: Colin
> Date: Sun, Jul 11, 2010 at 2:44 PM
> Subject:
> Re: Please
> To: Dan
>
> No, I wasn't too busy, didn't really have anything to say to you. Just that now I

feel I have to email you to let you know that your actions towards Mom and Megan are completely unacceptable. Mom is not going back to florida, ever. Megan does not want to go back there, but you want to make her do something she does not want to do. yet you say it's in someone else's hands, the courts i guess is what you think. totally false and a lie, you could easily let her stay in texas, what is what she wants. But your too self-centered and selfish to care about what Megan or anybody else wants for that matter, it's just all about you. You are creating this fight. Instead of letting things work themselves out or letting Meg decide what she wants to do. She's 14, she can make up her own mind. She is having panic and anxiety attacks just thinking of having to go back to florida by herself. why would that be? why would you want Megan to be in that state of feeling? fear and worry, panic and anxiety? and that is what will happen, as Mom said, she's not going back to florida. So Megan would have to be there by herself with you. So how do you think you'll take care of Megan by yourself? You'd really make Megan go to florida and stay in florida if she doesn't want to?! who does that? what kind of parent does that? what kind of husband treats his wife like you've treated Mom? who calls the cops on his wife and sister in law? ON HER BIRTHDAY!? who sends out disrespectful, contradictory, and impulsive irrational emails to family members telling your 'side' of the story? or emails completely annihilating Mom and not thinking there's any

> consequences to your actions? which anyone that knows this family and you and Mom could probably agree that how you characterize Mom is not anything remotely close to the truth, just your emotionally and psychologically impaired view of
> it. you need help dad, psychological and spiritual help and I hope you do eventually get it. Megan's taking cake decorating classes every Saturday now, for another 3 Saturdays. I guess if you make her go back, and it is you making her, no one else, she'll miss her last class, which she is really sad about. why are you forcing your will and your expectations and what you want to happen on everybody? I hope you decide to put Megan and her feelings before your own.

This is how I ended my response to Colin:

> For once, someone is putting Megan before themselves and that's me. Your Mom gave no thought at what she has done to Megan. Nor do you. It is the most selfish act I have ever witnessed, and you support it.
>
> I'm not letting Megan live without her father. Anne is the one who could resolve this by living close. I have the stable job and career, Megan is not going to live without a father. Her life, friends and school have been here.
>
> Miss her cake class Colin? Is that all you can define this down to? Megan was ripped from her home, her friends, counseling, swimming AND her father. I HAVE NOT SEEN HER FOR

OVER A MONTH!!

And you're extremely disappointed that she may miss her last cake class instead of possibly never seeing her father again????

This last statement sums up your whole position about this and me.

Dad

I also told Colin I would not be speaking with him any further about matters having to do with his mother or Megan as it was inappropriate, and that as one of our children, it was not a situation that he should be involved in. We could simply talk about other things. I was sad, but not surprised when I never heard from him again.

It was around this time that I noticed all of Megan's Facebook image galleries were gone. The countless selfies with her friends enjoying all sorts of activities - gone. In their place was one lonely image - Megan had taken a selfie of herself in a room of her Aunt Jean's home. She looked so small . . . just her image with a large vacant room behind her.

This was my defining moment. My devastation. The evidence that not only had I lost Meg but Megan had lost everything. She was stripped of her home, her friends, her social media . . . she was stripped of all that she knew.

With the divorce filing done and a petition in place to have Megan returned to Florida, Jamie Reed, Jean's husband contacted me via email:

Wed 7/21/2010 9:05 AM
From: Reed, Jamie
<JReed@TexasRangers.com> Re: Talk ASAP

Dan, I think you and I should talk asap and move this forward. Two lawyers times 300 dollars/hr is getting crazy. I do not have the emotional involvement that others might and want the best for everyone involved. I am in Detroit and tomorrow late morning-noon is good.

Jamie

I believed that Jamie didn't care about our daughter, and with all that had occurred I felt it best that he communicate through my sister, Dawn. She contacted Jamie and sent a summary of her conversation to me in the following email:

> From: Dawn
> Sent: Wednesday, July 21, 2010 2:07 PM
> To: Dan
> Subject: Conversation with Jamie Reed 07/21/10 approximately 9:30-10am
>
> Hi Danny,
> So....this morning I spoke with Jamie Reed (Jean's husband) who texted Danny yesterday asking Danny to call him.
>
> Points of Conversation:
>
> 1. Jamie hoping to resolve issues without further cost or at least as less as possible.
> 2. Jamie asked what did Dan want as Jamie is hoping for a resolution.
>   a. I told Jamie what Dan's two non-negotiable issues were:
>   b. Meggie is to be returned to Florida as soon as possible to attend high school in her current school district in FL.
>   c. Meggie should have access to BOTH Anne and Dan so Dan is willing to have a 50-50 custody split if Anne gets an apartment nearby.
>
> Jamie stated that Anne is not returning to Florida, so "3b" is not an option. I then told Jamie there are then really 3

options, which are:

1. Anne returns to FL, live separately from Dan (divorce) and they share 50-50 custody.
2. Anne relocates to TX, Dan stays in FL, and Meggie is with Danny.
3. Anne relocates to TX, Dan stays in FL, and Meggie is with Anne.

Jamie stated #1 is not an option. I stated # 3 is not an option. Jamie said Anne would be willing to do # 2, and send Meggie back to FL. I told Jamie the stipulation agreement has to be signed and submitted to both attorneys, with the marital property split (and Jamie and I agreed any marital property mediation could be done w/o attorneys).

Jamie did say that Anne does not care about the property, that Anne said Dan should take what he wants and Anne will look at everything left and choose from. I told Jamie, no, the marital property is to be split, no discussion as Danny was not going to just take what he wanted, nor was "anyone" going to just take what they wanted.

Jamie stated Anne is not well, she is under the care of a Dr and two counselors, and they are also advising Anne, according to Jamie, to not return to Florida.

Jamie said he hopes that one day, maybe 6 months down the road, a year down the road, maybe Anne will get healthy enough to want to return to FL and live by Meggie's school.

Jamie stated the marriage is definitely

over b/w Dan and Anne.

Jamie stated that he does believe we love Anne and Meggie. He stated his concern was Meggie too, and that if Dan really wanted Meggie, that Dan needs to be prepared of Meggie's condition. Jamie said Meggie has meltdowns, and that she is wetting the bed 5 nights a week. I reminded Jamie Meggie possibly wouldn't be going through all this if she had not be taken away from her father/Florida.

Jamie said, as Meggie's Aunt, that I should also think about the fact that he himself has heard Meggie say she did not want to live in Florida because she has cousins and a sister in TX. I reminded Jamie that Meggie's father is in FL, and no one takes precedent over her father or mother. I told Jamie Dan never heard from Meggie that she wanted to go to TX with Anne and Jean....it was done without approval.

Jamie stated that when Jean went to the house and the police were called, the police were already around the corner, and the police did in fact tell Anne and Jean it was best for them to go to TX. I told Jamie that I personally spoke to one of the officers as recent as 2 weeks ago and the officer said they (Anne and Jean) can go to TX, but they should not have taken Meggie.

Jamie repeatedly stated that we need to stay objective and neutral and not choose sides. Jamie even stated at one point he did not feel I was as objective as I could be. I told Jamie that this was not about Dan, or Anne, but about

Meggie, and making sure Meggie has access to both parents all the time, which is NOT currently happening.

I told Jamie that Danny would allow 24/7 access b/w Meggie and Anne via phone and internet. I also told Jamie that if Anne wanted to visit Meggie in FL, Danny would leave the residence and allow Anne to stay there during the visit (my guess is that Anne is being counseled to have zero contact with Danny). Jamie again stated Anne is not well, and that Dan needs to be prepared for Meggie's health issues. I told Jamie Meggie would return to counseling as Dan is not the one who discontinued her sessions.

Jamie stated Dan filed for divorce first, and I told Jamie Danny also got a text from Anne prior, stating it is over. Jamie said he was aware of Colin's email and confirmed Anne is never returning to FL. Jamie again stated the cost is mounting and he has friends that are attorneys and court costs could be quite expensive. Jamie also stated he would hate to see all the children be brought in by Anne's attorney to testify.
I told Jamie an attorney is just a hired person trying to win a case for their paying client. Jamie agreed, mentioned his attorney friends again, and then I told him I was aware of costs because not only is our President an attorney at my company, but we work with attorneys in DC everyday....that is what we do.

Jamie repeatedly would state we need to try and resolve all this and I mentioned I tried weeks ago by emailing Mrs. Wills 3 times. I also told Jamie that Bobbi and I were helping, and communicating with Anne up until a week before she went to TX, and Anne just stopped responding but that we were not just hearing one side of things. I also told Jamie it was strange that we all could communicate with Anne, but that not one person from the Wills side called Dan.

I told Jamie that Dan even had tried himself, before going to attorneys, to communicate with Anne over 40 times, but Anne would not respond back. Jamie said Anne was being advised by her two counsels, not to respond to Dan. I told Jamie then someone could have told Dan that as because of no response, Dan had to get the attorneys involved.

I told Jamie to please tell Anne and Meggie both, that we love them, and he said he would see them tomorrow, and tell Anne all that we spoke of. Jamie said again Anne is willing to send Meggie to FL. I told Jamie I would relay everything to Dan and Jamie asked me to email him my cell # and my email address.

Danny....PLEASE do not do anything until Jamie has a chance to get home tomorrow and speak with Anne. You will of course, want your attorney, per Donnie's stipulation and his recommendations, to review your proposal and think about any changes you may want to make.

A reminder.....you want whatever PET (S) returned too that Meggie wants to have with her in FL.

This is all a start of the end.....hopefully.

Dawn

Dawn sent the following confirmation and recap to Jamie of their discussion:

From: Dawn
Subject: Dawn's info
To: Jamie
Date: Wednesday, July 21, 2010, 2:49 PM

Hi Jamie,

I am glad we were able to talk today. My cell phone # is 443-956- 6007, home # is 410-672-0164. My email, since you will have received this, is of course - sdoshea@verizon.net.

I have communicated everything we spoke about to Dan and I have asked him to do nothing today, until you, Jamie, return home tomorrow and can speak with Anne.

I also communicated to Dan your concerns about Megan's health issues and Dan said he is prepared. I told Dan that you stated that Anne would be agreeable to sending Megan back to Florida as soon as possible.

Dan said again, the attorneys would have to have the stipulation papers signed in agreement, and he of course would set up all communication possible for Megan and Anne to communicate daily/whenever they chose, and of course Anne would have visits from Meggie in TX including some Holidays, some weekends, and some time in the summer.

> If Anne would like to go to FL and visit with Meggie, Dan would leave the residence and allow Megan and Anne to have their time together so Anne will not have to pay for a hotel. Dan would go to Bobbi's or to a hotel room to give Anne/Meggie time together.
>
> Also, we did not discuss....pets. Dan would like Meggie to bring the pets back to FL if that is what Meggie wants.
>
> Also, my sister and I would be available to assist Meggie, and hopefully the day will come soon that Anne is feeling better and would like to even visit with me. She could visit her friends in Maryland, and I have a car at her disposal. Anne is forever my sister.
>
> Praying for Anne, Dan, and Meggie, as well as Ryan, Colin, and Erin. I do love all of them.
>
> Thank you again Jamie and at least this is a start to a resolution.
> Please give Anne and Meggie my love when you see them.
>
> Dawn O'Shea

In a short time, Jamie came back with his response:

> From: Jamie
> Subject: RE: Dawn's info To: Dawn
> Date: Wednesday, July 21, 2010, 3:35 PM
>
> Dawn, that is not exactly what we talked about today. Megan has had complete melt downs worried that she would have to go back under those conditions. Obviously the best course for Megan at this point is the already agreed to

> Parental Evaluation and let the legal system run it's course since. I do want what is best for Megan and the parents but do not think the scenario presented here is it.
>
> Jamie

When I asked Dawn about Jamie's remark, "You don't want all of Danny's children testifying against him, do you?" Dawn relayed that portion of the conversation to me. "About what Jamie?" Dawn asked. Jamie responded, "Well, you know Danny has abused Anne his entire life." My sister doesn't yell when her anger gets going, she lowers her voice like our Mom. Extremely quiet and determined she said, "Jamie, you know that's not true." Jamie back-pedaled and responded, "Well, in the last several years."

Again, my sister said to him, "Jamie, you know Danny never abused Anne and never would, and how could you know, you haven't seen Danny in almost twenty years." Jamie went silent; it was the end of any negotiation. I was left with the threat that my own children would falsely accuse me in a court of law. It was also hard to comprehend my wife's own mother allowing such assertions, when just a year earlier I received the following card from her:

> I'm grateful that you are my son, Dan. Thank you for working so hard and faithfully caring for your family. I KNOW your Dad and Rol are watching over you and are pleased with you...so is our heavenly Father.
>
> love you Mom

As I was in the early stages of Parental Alienation I had no idea what it was, or that it was an actual syndrome. On July 28, 2010, my sister Dawn sent me information on PAS. I read it and quickly realized that it was what I was going through with Anne. I put it aside at the time, believing the legal system would protect our daughter's relationship with both of her parents. I was so naïve. My sister's email:

From: Dawn
Subject: PAS attachment : Meggie
OShea To: Dan
Date: Wednesday, July 28, 2010, 8:45
AM

Danny,
EXCELLENT article the paralegal told me about on PAS (Parental Alienation Syndrome) !!!!! I have attached it for everyone to read.
Stay calm, work is a must, and remember:
Your job allows you to work from home if Meggie is sick/home from school.
What is best for Meggie...is both parents and you are promoting a relationship with both parents and Meggie....different from Anne.
In the attached article...Anne is the AP (alienating parent)...you are the TP (targeted parent).
Tell your counselor you are reading trying to understand what Meggie is going through and ask your counselor about PAS.
Meggie....this article gives examples of a child's symptoms.....so Meggie's melt downs and bed wetting (if what Jamie wrote and said is true), may very well be symptoms of PAS. Ask Robyn.
Excellent, informative reading attached....
XXXOOO, D.

My sister Dawn, Megan's aunt, was closer to her than any of her other aunts, including those on Anne's side. They emailed and spoke countless times. The following are a few of the many communications they had over the years, before Parental Alienation separated them too:

From: Megan

Subject: Re: Crate for Puppy To:
sdoshea@verizon.net
Date: Friday, October 24, 2008, 3:35
PM

Aunt Dawn,
Hey! I got the book puppies for dummies! It is a great book so far! If you look through the pictures of the puppies, you might see a papillon. That is the type of dog we are looking at! I am keeping tabs in the book at VERY helpful parts.
That's practically the whole book! i have found the section about how to introduce the puppy to the cat the most helpful, since we really worried about how Meeshee will take it, but with these tips I'm sure meeshee will be just fine after a while! I am very excited and can't wait! We were concerned about who was going to watch her while we were at swim meets but I have THREE backup people, and they have all had expriences with dogs! We are thinking up names for her and so far we like Lily and Mille, but I am leaning toward Millie! if you have any ideas, please email me! I love you so much! You have been such a big help!
love, Meggie xoxo

On Tue, Oct 14, 2008 at 8:43 AM,
From: Dawn

Meggie,

Crates can cost up to $60 for a small dog but you can usually find them used in the sell sections of newspapers. For piece of mind, seriously think about crate training...it is a SAFE place for a puppy, esp at nite while everyone is

sleeping, and also especially when all of you are not home.
Your Uncle Donnie dated a girl in high school named Shelly Hall. She got a small puppy. Every time they went out, they put the puppy in the basement. They went to dinner one nite and went to let the puppy out of the basement, and the puppy CHEWED on a plug to a lamp that was plugged into the wall and puppy got electrocuted and died.
Piece of mind and puppy's safety should always come first (even though you want the puppy in the bed with you). The puppy will get in the bed....later. Just only ...after...he or she has learned what to chew and what not to chew.
When you think it is time to start leaving her out of the crate, you just go outside your door for a few minutes at a time. Then maybe 20 min, to rake, yard work, clean out car, etc. Then you do it for an hour (maybe a quick run to the store).
It is very very important to let the puppy know ....very strongly....if they chew on something they shouldn't, then you immediately show them what they can chew. Be careful of rawhides...only give when you are watching them. When they get a small piece torn off, throw it away.
Rawhide can choke them, and it can also block a bowl movement for a week!
Remember, they are a puppy, and they really do not understand anything until they are about 16- 20 weeks old. You discipline but keep in mind again, they really don't comprehend until 16-20 weeks old.
There is a GREAT book called "Puppies for Dummies" (yes, it is part

of the for Dummies series). I have it
and learned so very much!!!!!
Please get it and read!!!! XO, D.
From: Megan To: Dawn

Subject: Re: And her name is...
Date: Monday, October 13, 2008, 3:54 PM

Hey crazy aunt dawn! thats so cool! i cant wait to see a picture of her! Crabcake is such a cute name! My mom and dad are looking at papillons (dog) for Christmas! i am so excited! I love ya! give chesapeake, cambridge AND crabcake love for me!
luv, meggie
ps. i don't know if you have these pictures but here they r anyway! they r of me and you, me and the pups and me and colin!

From: Megan
Subject: puppy!
To: Dawn
Date: Saturday, November 29, 2008, 9:22 PM

Hey Aunt Dawn! I am so excited today I picked out my puppy! She is so..... CUTE! I love her so... MUCH! Only two more weeks until she moves home! YAY! Here are some pictures of her! By the way I was wondering what the name of the conditioner was. We have EVERYTHING except for that. Oh my gosh I am just so excited! She is the littlest of the litter and that is why i love her! She is so... SWEET! Our Christmas picture is going to be me and Sophie!

Thank you again! You have helped us so much! I love you! Love,
Meggie, Sophie

From: Dawn Subject: Re: puppy!
To: Megan
Date: Monday, December 1, 2008, 8:07 AM

I LOVE HER !!!! SHE IS ADORABLE !!!!
I'm so happy for you and Ryan both !!!!! WELCOME to its a dogs world!!!! Yes, I'm working on my Christmas card now too!
There are two sprays, and let me correct myself, as they are NOT conditioners. They are anti itch sprays (which basically replenishes the oils in dogs' coats as bathing strips the oils dogs need).
One is "DERMCARE anti itch spray" (available at PETSMART).
The other, which is what I use, I got from my vet, and it is called "Derma-Soothe" anti itch spray.
Either one of these is great, esp b/w bathing. My dogs love it as after spraying, you brush them. My dogs tackle me and fight to get the most brushing.
My dogs get bathed once a month, and sprayed every ten days w/ the anti itch spray. I think Sophie is too cute!!!!!!!!
I'm so happy and excited for you.
And remember, after puppy pees outside, she needs to go every 45 min...otherwise accidents occur. If she circles carpet/floor while sniffing....she also needs to go out. Keep me posted!!!!

As July 2010 came to a close, I was beyond excited that Megan would be returning soon. The deadline was August 11th and I had no doubt that Anne and Jean would keep her until the final day. Hagerty High School had their freshman orientation prior to Megan's return and I had to attend without her. It was such a punch in the gut to see parents with their excited children heading into the next stage of their lives.

I was removing my wife's email from the server - since she no longer used it - when I noticed that my wife had her Facebook posts sent to her email. On August 10, 2010 a post came through from my third child, Erin:

> Jean said this started maybe 50 days ago wen really started when they met BUT beg. of april I KNEW i felt it that if somehow i picked up that phone and called my mom or dad something was wrong I KNEW IT I FELT IT. the lord said ERIN WAIT BE PATIENT YOU WILL FIND OUT SHORTl.Y AND DO NOT BE MAD AT FINDING OUT NOW. and you know what i waited and waited and knew and finally it was driving me aazy i needed to hear my moms voice i had to hear my sisters. i still havent talked to my mom but jean i know told her everything we talked abt and to let her know this is NOT MY MOMS FAULT. AT ALL I KNOW ITS NOT IF I COULD DESCRIBE ONE WORD FOR HER ITS. SAINT. SHE IS MY ANGEL AND SHE did was she
> was told to do by the lord. the lord said ok i have to take dan to hell and change this and its time for megan to be a child and play and not be an adult when shes 14. so the lord took them away from dan

Erin moved to South Carolina with Anne, Megan, and I in 2004, then went on to Texas several years later to be near her cousins, Becky and Rachel, Jean and Jamie's children. As teenagers often do, she became irresponsible and stopped meeting some of her financial obligations to her Aunt Jean. As a consequence, Anne and I decided to give her the car that we had been letting her use so that she would have to pay the insurance on her own.

Around 2007 Erin cut off all contact with Anne and me. It wasn't until 2009, shortly before we moved to Florida, that Erin reconnected with her mother, still remaining silent with me. Periodically Anne would hand the phone to me, leaving us to share short, uncomfortable conversations.

The words in the Facebook post were shocking; "take dan to hell" and along with it, the final judgment: "so the lord took them away from dan."

This wasn't a scourge by the heavens above. This "judgment" and "hell" was created by human hands, by lies and deception. This is what alienators and enablers do. And they used a child to do it; they used Megan to do it.

It isn't just the emotional and psychological aspects of Parental Alienation that brings trauma when a child is taken, but it affects physical well-being too. When I accepted the new position in Orlando and moved from South Carolina, I couldn't work out as I used to. I loved to run along the beach of Isle of Palms but the new department I was creating left little time to exercise. I gained forty pounds and weighed 230 pounds when Meg was taken in June of 2010. I couldn't eat, I couldn't keep food down. In those two months Megan was gone I lost those forty pounds.

On August 11, 2010, my sisters Bobbi and Dawn (who had flown in from Maryland) and I met Meg at the Fort Lauderdale Airport. Jean was the one who dropped Megan off, Anne wasn't there. Jean looked at me with fire in her eyes. It was sad and uncomfortable. I wonder how it made Megan feel. Thirty-plus years as a family and now we couldn't even be cordial, not even for Megan's sake.

When Megan, my sisters and I arrived at the home where Megan lived before she was taken, I sat on the sofa with Megan. With me next to her and Sophie on her lap, a picture was snapped. I will treasure the picture all the days of my life – the day she returned. We learned that Megan hardly had any clothes with her. Anne and Jean had given her very little for her return to begin her freshman year in high school.

Without hesitation, Megan's Aunt Dawn immediately took it upon herself to take Meg on a shopping spree for clothes for high school. It was fun to listen to the shopping stories and what they looked for and what they bought. Megan gave me a full fashion show of all that she and Dawn had bought, returning in a full change of clothes, or returning in different combinations as I took pictures of each!

Within a couple days of being home, Megan asked me if she could spend the night at her best friend Lizzie's house, asking almost as if I wouldn't let her, the result of her "programming." Little did she know that for two months my constant plea and cry in prayer was her return to her friends and the life she knew. I had to work and couldn't get off before she wanted to be there as it involved a number of her friends so her Aunt Dawn dropped her off at her best friend's house.

When I returned home from work Dawn shared how happy Meg had been to see her friends:

> "*You should have seen her Danny, she was so happy! When I pulled up to the house, Lizzie was waiting for her with a bunch of other girls. They all came running out laughing and hugging Meg. It was so sweet. Meg introduced me and the girls turned, walking back to the house arm in arm. Danny, all I can describe by the look on Meg's face was*" – her voice cracked – "*pure joy.*"

We both sat there and cried. Megan should have been enjoying her friends all year 'round, not living in Texas for two months isolated from her normal daily life. It broke my heart.

Later that evening, my sisters and I were invited over with other parents for refreshments at the back porch pool. The girls played in and out of the pool as they used to, as I remembered. They were in their own world, in their own element. Just seeing Meg back with the friends she loved, in her own world, not with me, not with her mother, just being who she was, it was a defining moment. The other parents and my sisters and I briefly talked about Megan being taken. Megan's best friend's father told us the parents believed Megan was never coming back.

Shortly after Megan's return, we moved from the home we had shared as a family before Megan was taken. I found a wonderful three-bedroom apartment in a gated complex. One bedroom was for me, and the two others were for Meg. One to sleep in, the other was her "entertainment room," complete with a pull-out sofa bed, TV, and electronic keyboard.

For the first few days after moving in, Meg and I painted her rooms in the colors she had chosen - a Melon Extract (dark green) on one side, an Apple Green (light green) on another, and pink on a smaller area by the sink in her bathroom between the rooms. We ordered a flower carpet with different colors, a lamp with 4 different shade colors, and more.

One night we painted for 5 hours straight, working and listening to Meg's music together. We almost had her room finished by the time I took her to her friend's house for the evening. When I picked her up I told Megan I'd be going to work early and would get home around 4 o'clock the next day. Meg had her best friend's birthday sleep over and said she'd be leaving around 2 p.m. Then, realizing what that meant, in a very disappointed tone Megan said, "*Ohhh, then I won't see you tomorrow?*"

Life is funny. She was disappointed, I should have been disappointed . . . yet her tone and statement had me walking on air for the rest of the night and the next day. Megan was "*disappointed*" that she wouldn't see me! I told her I was off Sunday and that we would spend the whole day together.

We finished painting Megan's rooms a few days later. Every so often I looked over at Meg, dreadfully afraid she was the ghost I had been seeing over the previous two months, on the couch doing her homework or sitting on the brick fence in the back yard or walking with her friends, always fading away again.

Meg didn't see me, but instinctively I took a picture with my cell phone, not a clear one, but one that settled the fears I still had under the psychological weight of Parental Alienation; she was still there painting, no longer a ghost . . . she didn't fade away this time.

She remained.

c.1962 - c.1964; Me with my older sister Bobbi, younger sister Dawn and my brother Donnie.

Left: c.1960 - c.1964; Mom and Dad. I couldn't ask for better parents.
Right: 1975; Anne and I at the Jesus '75 Festival. Our first months together.

c.1976 - c.1977; Anne and I in our first years of dating.

July 21, 1979; Our wedding day. "In the marriage of Anne Wills & Daniel O'Shea."

Left: July 21, 1979; Our wedding day "Limo Shot." **Right**: 1979; Anne and I biked frequently in our first 5 years. An early 'selfie.'

Left: August 1980; My Dad and me. Within a month he passed away. **Right**: March 20, 1981; The birth of my first son, Ryan.

c.1978 - c.1980; Anne's sister and brothers, Katie, Paul and David. I came to love them as if my own sister and brothers.

c.1982; My first son Ryan. I loved taking him to the field nearby our home. This picture was taken on one of those treasured days.

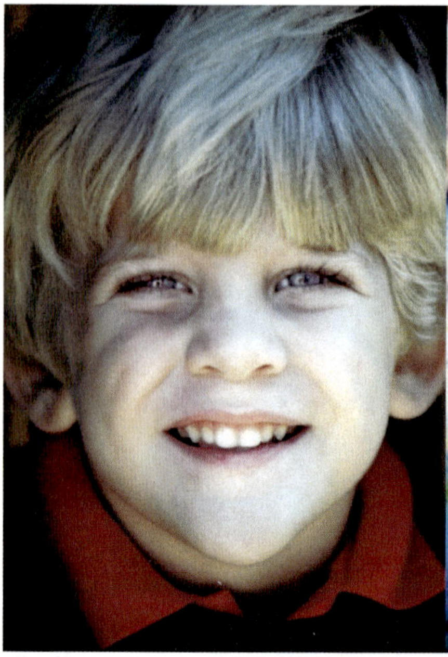

Left: c.1987 - c.1988; With Colin at the park, I captured a favored shot.
Right: c.1988 - c.1989; Here I caught Erin's 'big brown eyes.'

Left: c.1988 - c.1989; Our first annual Christmas shot at the 'park wall.'
Right: c.1988; Erin and me. One of my favorite pictures.

c.1990 - c.1991; One of my favorite pictures of our children. Ryan, Erin and Colin. Their facial expressions captured their personalities.

Left: c.1993; Our annual Christmas card picture at the 'park wall.'
Right: c.1994; Our continuing annual Christmas picture.

Left: c.1995; Our annual Christmas picture on the 'park wall.'
Right: c.1999; Megan with her little "Kitty." She was never without her.

Fall, 1996; Our annual Christmas picture on the 'park wall.' Megan was our new addition that year.

c.1997; Our annual Christmas picture at the 'park wall.' The wall hasn't changed much, but we have.

c.1999; Our Christmas picture through the years. Approximately ten years of the annual trip to the 'park wall.'

c.1999; Summertime I'd be up getting cereal ready before work. Almost every day I'd hear Meg's little footsteps coming down to join me.

c.2000; Our four children at home in Baltimore, Maryland.

c.2000; Anne and me after over twenty years of marriage. She was always beautiful to me.

c.2000-2001; Our last Christmas picture on the 'park wall.'

Left: c.2001; Megan dressed up as Madeline.
Right: Spring, 2004; Erin before her high school prom.

c.2006; Ryan with his dog Jules at the Isle of Palms, South Carolina dog show.

c.2005; Colin training to fly Chinook helicopters in the army.

c.2004; Our annual Christmas picture, taken on Seabrook Island, South Carolina.

Spring, 2006; Megan at the Charleston, SC city championship swim meet. It was in the water where her healing from high anxiety syndrome began.

Fall, 2006; Megan at swim practice shortly after beginning to swim for the Mount Pleasant year-round swim team.

Fall, 2006; Our annual Christmas picture at Isle of Palms, South Carolina.

c.2007; Megan on the day we picked up her new papillon puppy, Sophie. When Meg was last taken to Texas, I never saw Sophie again either.

c.2007; Megan was becoming an accomplished year-round swimmer. Here in her favorite stroke – the butterfly.

c.2008; Our annual Christmas picture taken on Isle of Palms, South Carolina. It would be our last Christmas picture ever taken.

c.2010; Megan created such artistic image galleries. When she was taken, she was not allowed to speak with her friends in Florida during the first month.

August 11, 2010; The day Meg returned after taken two months before. A day I thought at times would never come. I lost 40 lbs., I couldn't eat.

Fall, 2010; Meg with Aunt Dawn. Growing up, Dawn was her favorite Aunt. All contact was cut off from her too after being taken the last time.

Spring, 2010; One of Meg's last events as a Junior Olympic Swimmer. After being taken the first time to Texas, she never swam again.

Fall, 2015; With my brother Donnie and sisters Dawn and Bobbi. I couldn't imagine getting through PAS without them.

Meg - when she and I would be silly and play around together. It's how I'll always remember her.

Chapter 11

Goodbyes –
Goodbye Meg, I Love You Very Much

"And they wonder, as waiting the long years through,
In the dust of that little chair,"

When Megan was first taken, I assumed that if divorce was the final destination, the dust would settle and sanity would prevail. I believed that the worst was behind us and that if nothing else the courts would act in protection of all of us. Anne's right to be a mother, mine to be a father, and most importantly, Megan's given right at birth to be our daughter, I believed that it would all be protected.

I think I also hoped that with Megan settling back into a normal life with her friends and activities, Anne and her family would embrace her happiness and allow her to continue living in the environment she had been a part of for most of her childhood. With only a few years of high school ahead of her it would have been . . . should have been easy for Anne to stick it out in Florida until Meg graduated.

I couldn't have been more wrong.

Anne came back to live in Florida, and attorneys came onto the scene. We went to mediation and at first Anne wouldn't agree to anything. She wouldn't even agree to meet in the same room. Our mediation took place with her in one room, me in another and my attorney going back and forth. The issues were temporary support and child sharing.

With respect to child sharing, Anne wanted custody and would let me "have Megan every other weekend." She further demanded that I leave our home (at this point she was unaware that I had moved into an apartment) and stay in a hotel when she had Megan. So basically, if she got her way, I was to live in a hotel 26 days of the month and on my weekends, I could live in my home. Fortunately Florida has a law which supports joint custody and 50/50 parenting. The end result at that point, Megan would alternate between Anne and me every other week.

On my weeks, I spent as much time as I could with Meg. There was a school bus that stopped right at our apartment complex, but Meg wanted me to take her to school. To me that was just a little more time we could spend together. It was a daily 20-minute roundtrip that I cherished. Every other Monday began a week of silence, a week I did not want nor could I ever get used to. The "every other week" goodbyes.

I would take her to school on Anne's Monday morning . . . "*Goodbye Meg, I love you very much.*" I would sit there and watch her walk all the way into school, knowing, most times, that I would not hear from her the entire coming week. No phone call, no email. That was our life for the entire school year. Beyond not hearing from Megan I also did not know where she was going. Anne refused to give me the address of their new home.

Sadly, Megan no longer swam. As her mother and I had always agreed to, I made sure that Megan participated in an afterschool activity. Instead of swimming, Megan said she wanted to play Lacrosse with her friends. I was ecstatic. Perfect! I was happy she found something that made her happy and kept her active. After several months of those Mondays - "*Goodbye Meg, I love you very much,*" she came back from her time with her mother and I found out she had stopped playing Lacrosse "Why aren't you playing Lacrosse any more Meg? I thought you loved it?" No answer. Just silence. I tabled the topic; not wanting to make Meg feel bad, I thought it best to let it go.

With all of my children I always tried going to their afterschool activities, sports, concerts, talent shows or anything they participated in. I wasn't always afforded that luxury now with Meg, not because I didn't want to attend but because I wasn't invited. I would find out after the fact that Megan had an after-school performance when she was in her Mom's care. I wouldn't ask her why I wasn't told, I assumed it was because of Anne not wanting me there. What other reason could there be?

One night during the first semester of Megan's freshman year, I received an unexpected call from Megan. She needed a paper printed for school the next day, but the couple they were living with "went to bed early" and she couldn't use their printer. It was then that I found out Megan and her mother were sleeping in one bedroom of a home they shared with another couple. I gave Megan every choice I could think of, have her mother drive her over to the apartment where Megan could use the computer I had set up for us, or I could pick her up. There was no option, Anne didn't want me to have their address and she didn't want to drive her to me. Megan just said in exasperation, *"I'll figure it out."* I was learning the crushing symptoms of Parental Alienation, as a parent who wanted to help his child, but couldn't. Her words echo even now, *"I'll figure it out."*

It was around the middle of October when I felt it was time to say something to Meg. Anne and Jean began a campaign about the Texas Rangers, Colin had added multiple Facebook posts about the Rangers (never cared before), Erin's post "See you in five weeks...whooo-hooo." Jean's daughter Rachel was getting married around Thanksgiving and Meg was going to join in the festivities. Under normal circumstances I would have been nothing but happy to see Meg go and enjoy her Mom's side of the family. She was excited to visit Texas, and although I was happy for her, I was frightened for us. I was fearful of the growing emotional distance that was taking hold as a result of the way her time was spent when she was with her Mom.

On top of my fears I found out that Megan knew about her Mom's relocation motion. Megan's maternal grandmother would frequently send her letters. Letters that I would place on Meg's bed - unopened as they should have been. One day as I went to get the mail, several pieces dropped to the ground. There was a rosary too bulky and large for the packaging that it was in, and as a result the envelope split open when it hit the ground, spilling all of its contents. I picked up the rosary, the envelope, and the card. As if the words were blinking in bright neon lights, I saw the following; "When you will be in Texas permanently…"

I wondered how Meg was functioning with the knowledge she was keeping from me. I wondered how she felt having to keep secrets from me for her mother. I began to understand why she was pulling away from me. It was during this period that she began locking herself in her room immediately after dinner. Ordinarily we would have watched TV together, or talked, done schoolwork . . . something. Now she was locking her bedroom door . . . locking herself in and me out. I knew I had to talk with her. I also knew I had to be careful not to place her further in the middle.

I sat Meg down and began speaking, measuring my words carefully. You see, now I could not simply speak my mind with my own child, as one of the laws used to determine custody was whether a parent spoke of the legal issues with the child. The courts were now listening in:

> "The capacity and disposition of each parent to protect the child from the ongoing litigation as demonstrated by not discussing the litigation with the child, not sharing documents or electronic media related to the litigation with the child, and refraining from disparaging comments about the other parent to the child."

So I began my talk with Megan:

> "Megan, you only called me once from Wednesday until Sunday. I called you a number of times. This is unacceptable and I do expect to hear from you and want to know how you're doing.
>
> Also, you're locking the doors for the first time ever. You know we've never locked doors in our home and we're not starting now. I've never barged in without knocking and hearing you say, "Come in" or you coming to the door and that's not going to change.
>
> After you told me your mother was going to the Texas-Tampa game, you know you could have gone with her even if you were with me this week. I would have driven you there if you wanted to go and enjoy the game with your Mom.
>
> Your Mom and I are in disagreement as to where you will live for most of the year. Up until recently, she wanted you in Texas during the school year and you would only come here for the summers. This isn't fair to you for two reasons:

One, you'd be here the entire summer in an apartment with very few friends left while I worked until 6 p.m. That's not fair to you. Two, during the school year I'd see you only two days per month, twenty days in ten months excluding some holidays. That doesn't work. I'm not going to live seeing you just two days a month for a number of months during the school year. Further, your school schedule works with my work schedule.

I'm not going to ask you where you want to live because you shouldn't have to choose. But I will tell you this, I will never take you away from your mother and you should never be taken away from me. I will never ask you that question. There are too many things other people will look at, as this is no longer your mother's or my decision. You will be living where it is best for you.

I also am not going to live as I did when you were in Texas for those two months. It was the worst two months I have ever lived. You were not answering your cell phone or responding to email and I know for a fact that other people were allowed access and had control. Whether you are here in Florida or in Texas I will to the best of my ability, make sure you have unlimited and private access set up for both your Mom and me.

I am and will go to the ends of the earth to fight for equal time with you. I love you too much not to. In the next three years, you will need support from both your mother AND your father.

I am the one your brothers and sister turned to for certain things. I taught each of your brothers and sister how to drive. When their grades faltered, I instilled in them the importance of their education. When they needed support in their after-school activities I gave them advice on what to do, drove and picked them up, and watched as many events as I could. For twenty-nine years I had at least one of you under my roof, and I don't, if I can help it, expect this to change until you are of age.

The day you were taken away was the worst day of my life - that includes the days my Mom and Dad died.

During your remaining school years, I will do everything to prevent the circumstance that when you need and turn to your father I won't be there. I will walk to the ends of the earth to prevent that from happening.
Each one of you were and are my joy and job in life and I expect to finish it.
I never told you this, but when I was 9 or 10 years old living with my Mom and Dad in Connecticut, I used to cry myself to sleep in a drenched pillow soaked by tears after praying in anguish that nothing would happen to my Mom or Dad.

My worst fear has occurred to you.

You know that our rule, your mother's and mine, was that you had to participate in something, no matter if it was swimming or any other after-school activity. Always your choice. You loved swimming. I was disappointed when you went to Texas and stopped swimming, because I don't believe it was YOUR choice. At first you were the one who told me you wanted to practice with the swim team out there and I told you I would even pay for it. Then it changed to Jean was going to swim and practice with you. Then it ended abruptly and you never gave me a reason why you no longer wanted to swim.

Ryan, Colin and Erin never went to college. You had a gift in swimming and my real disappointment for you was in the manner that swimming ended.

You yourself before being taken away logged into USA Swimming almost nightly, proud of your swim times comparing them with Florida and National times. I looked at it as an accomplishment for you and a door to a scholarship to a college education and degree an opportunity your brothers and sisters never had.

You wanted to learn to bake instead. Now, you no longer bake.

You wanted to play Lacrosse, now you don't. I am gravely concerned about your future and lack of interests.

Lastly, I know people in our family have made comments about me, and that they have done so without any direct knowledge of my side of things, or of what really happened between your mom and me.

I will only tell you this: Some people in our family have never given me the respect or the common decency to talk to me about what they have been told.

> They believe what they hear from someone else instead of coming straight to me. If anyone, family or friends tells you something negative about me, or tells you something negative that I have said, please come and ask me. I will respectfully give you the truth; you may not like what I have to say, but at least have the respect to ask.
>
> One of the worst things people can engage in is talking about someone behind their back. It is wrong to not allow a person to respond or defend themselves. I am asking you to not allow anyone else to say I did things or said things that I cannot respond to. It is disrespectful and wrong.
>
> I love you very much Meg.

As Megan went back to her room – without locking the door – I thought of the time earlier that year when she was blossoming like a flower with school, friends and swimming. Now my little girl was being swallowed up in turmoil. Now her future was uncertain. Now she was caught in the middle of a battle that should not be occurring. A completely unnecessary battle. A battle that would eventually alienate her not only from the life she knew but also from her entire paternal family. PAS really is FAS. Family Alienation Syndrome.

As I was fighting to be my daughter's father, another fight was in play between my son Colin and his cousin Bethany (Bobbi's daughter). Colin's email:

> Nov 1, 2010, at 4:15 AM
> Colin O'Shea
>
> o what's the Deal-io Beth?! you de-friend a nephew?! you don't believe in communication like my Dad? So you're taking his "side" (by "side" i mean narcissistic psychologically skewed reality) of course i imagine? Based on

> what? Have you spoken to Ryan, Me, Erin, Megan, or,Hmmm, HIS WIFE to see what the reality of the situation is? The fact of the matter is that it is us that are in the middle of it and don't you think that the fact that his children are condemning his behavior is proof enough that his actions are despicable? And let's see, hmmm, he doesn't want to support in any way shape or form his wife of 31 years, financially? fighting every step of the way to NOT help her with the measly 1100 he gives her a month? Pathetic... beyond Measure.. And posting ridiculous stuff on facebook (which is beyond immature), already saying he's single, and he's the good guy? please, join the rest of us in reality.... Please, get real, Pathetic.

When I received this from Dawn, I realized it was all worse than I ever imagined. Forget the fact that the court did indeed set the financial support, here was my son, I was his dad for his whole life, and suddenly - or not so suddenly - he had forgotten who I was and how I loved him, his brother, his sisters and his mother.

Megan went to be with her mother for the week. I sent the following email to my sisters and brother:

> From: Dan
> Sent: Friday, November 5, 2010 10:26 AM
> To: Dawn, Bobbi, Donnie, Bethany
> Subject: Megan
>
> Have not heard from Megan all week. I assume in the aftermath of Colin and heading towards their Thanksgiving trip they've said or done something...again.

I did not know until after I lost Megan permanently that my niece Bethany had responded to Colin's Facebook message. Bethany's response to Colin wasn't just a mere moment of wisdom but a response from her own experience of being a former child of Parental Alienation. Her father took her at the age of 7 and her brother Marc at the age of 12 and hid them for months from their mother, my sister Bobbi. Bethany's email:

> Colin,
>
> Before I respond to your "message" let me make one thing clear before we go any further. You will NOT ever speak to me in an email or message in that tone ever again if you want to keep the lines of communication open. I am a 36 yr old MOTHER of 3 and a wife of 14 years. More importantly, I am a child of divorce who was, like your sister Megan, taken across the country from one of her parents. I, better than most, know more about this kind of situation than even you do. I LIVED IT. So the next time you address me or want to send me an email, do so w/ a little more respect. Not only do I deserve it, I have earned it.
>
> First, let me correct one of your many assumptions in your message. I did delete you and your brother and sisters as my friends on facebook. But not for the reason you may think. I was absolutely SICK AND DISGUSTED by the childish rantings and ravings of your sister Erin. Her "pathetic" (to use a word you seem to like) distortions of scripture and outright abusive words and threats towards her father on a daily basis, were not only offensive to me and my family, but they were tacky and classless. Aren't we better than that? Doesn't our family name deserve better

than to be drug in the mud all over facebook by a twenty-something angry little girl? Have some class and taste and GUTS and call your father Erin! And if your too afraid to do that, then send an email and let him know what you think or how you feel. Don't DISGRACE our family by humiliating yourself and your father all over facebook. So, yes, I deleted her and in turn felt it best if I deleted all of you so I did not have to see on your pages or on my news feed all of her comments to you about this sad situation. Not only did I feel this was best for my peace of mind, but also didn't think Megan (who is a child) needed to be witness to the nastiness that this has all become. I knew that if you wanted or needed to talk to me you would message me.

Second, in response to "have I spoken to Ryan, Me, Erin, Megan, or Hmmmm, HIS WIFE to see what the reality of the situation is?" Be careful how you proceed here, Colin. That question reeks of hypocrisy. I will pose the same question to you and Erin. Have YOU EVER TRIED CALLING YOUR FATHER? Don't bother answering that. I know you haven't just from what you stated above. IF you had called your dad, you would be singing a different tune. EVERY story has three sides usually, Colin. His, hers and the TRUTH. Even if you believe everything your mother and your Aunt Jean have told you, why haven't you called your father? Even if it was to yell at him for the "despicable" actions of his? Doesn't he deserve to have a say? You have already tried and judged and sentenced him w/out hearing his side. I expect this kind of behavior from Erin. She has proven herself time and again to be a bitter and angry person who needs help. But you, I expected more and BETTER from you.

SO, I pose this question to you...enlighten me because I want to know. And I am being serious and honest....I want to know...what has your father done? Please tell me the awful things he has done to warrant his children vilifying him? I have sat up many a night and racked my brain as to what terrible things he must have done. I have wanted to on many occasions email you and ask you but did not feel it was my place. And yes, I do only know one side as you put it. Your father's. I have never been close enough w/ your mother to just call her up and say, "so Anne, what in the world is going on w/ you and Danny?" You should know that and for you to suggest I do so, is ridiculous. But I have felt close enough w/ you but I never felt it was my place. But you have put me here, so now I ask....what has he done? Tell me. Maybe I will have a different perspective. But, if I can be so bold as to ask you to do the same. Call your father. Ask him what in the world is going on. Even if you want to yell and scream, give him the time of day and respect he deserves as your father to tell his side of the story. I guarantee you, you will be surprised to find out that your mother is not being honest. There is a lot more to all of this than you know. That might hurt to hear, but it is the absolute truth.

I will not address the above mentioned "measly 1100" a month except to say this, you don't know the entire story. Call your father if you want to know. I am sure however, that your mother and Aunt Jean will dissuade you from calling your dad b/c they know that there is a whole lot you will discover in talking to him and your eyes will be opened and your heart just might be changed. Regardless of what you decide to do, just know that no matter what words you might of said about your father, to him, etc..he will always love you. And he will forgive you for how you have treated him. And you can forgive him too.

Do you want to spend the rest of your life w/ out him? Trust me...don't make decisions you can't take back. I have not seen my father since I was 7 years old. He chose not to be a part of my life after he kidnapped my brother and me and was caught. But even w/ all the awful stuff he did, I still wanted him in my life. And my mother never said a bad word about him to me. EVER.

I will respect and love your father forever for fighting to keep Megan in his life no matter what. My father never did. I know he loves her. He wants what is best for her.

I will end w/ a few things...first, even though through these emails, we might disagree and be angry w/ one another, I am ALWAYS HERE FOR YOU. I have walked this road and I know you are in the middle and it is awful. If you

> ever need me I am here. Second, above all things my main concern is for Megan. NOT Anne and not even Danny. They are adults and can speak for themselves. Megan is a child and I want what is best for her. And lastly, and please listen carefully...if you have any love for you father at all and have disregarded all I have said in this lengthy email, then please hear this..your father is hurting. He has lost over 40lbs and has had chest pains. Call him. Tell him you love him. Check on him. He has called your aunt Dawn many times crying and telling her he still loves his wife. Those are not the actions of a malicious person. He misses his kids and doesn't deserve the hell is being put through. Call him and get his side of the story. You owe him that.
>
> Bethany

Colin never called me.

The holidays came for the first time for a family no longer together. As in all shared- custody, holidays are split. Thanksgiving came and Megan would be with her mother, on a trip to Texas. Christmas came and Megan would be with me. I looked forward to Meg, me and my extended family enjoying time together, as Meg enjoyed time with her mother's family in Texas. We went to visit my sister Bobbi in Ocala, Florida – Bobbi and her husband Tom, and my sister's daughter Bethany along with her husband Jake and their kids.

I watched Megan and she didn't smile much, not the beautiful smile she used to have. There were moments of shuffleboard together and her with her cousins watching movies, but Christmas morning with everyone around the Christmas tree opening presents, she seldom smiled. Late Christmas day, as twilight set in, I went for a long walk and cried for Meg, for my little girl.

It was shortly after Christmas that Anne informed me by email that she lost her "job" cleaning for a family and would be returning to Texas

- and that I would have to keep Megan for an extra week. I then realized why Megan didn't smile that much at Christmas; the child projects what the alienator feels, while the alienated projects what the child feels.

Anne returned several weeks later and the visitation schedule resumed. Anne had moved and once again I was not informed as to where Megan would be living every other week.

Shortly thereafter, I learned where Megan went during her weeks with her mother. Jamie and Jean had registered Anne at an extended stay hotel in Oviedo at $1,600 per month (my 3-bedroom apartment was $1,200; they could have easily provided Meg a home instead of a hotel). I could see in my mind's eye Megan walking Sophie, her little papillon, morning and nights, around strangers and transients at a hotel. It crushed me. It scared me.

As is the case with many children going through the upheaval of divorce, Megan's grades began to drop from A's and B's to B's and C's. I had to become vigilant to stay on top of her homework and projects. I kept a watchful eye on when they were due, and did what I could to ensure they were completed and turned in. Unfortunately, I could only support Megan's schoolwork on the weeks she spent in my home. I communicated with her teachers every week and attempted to schedule several parent-teacher conferences with Anne. Sadly, she would not cooperate . . . she would not show up.

My sister Dawn had arranged to come and visit Meg and I for a week. Megan was looking forward to the visit, and then suddenly on the eve that Dawn was flying in, she asked to sleep at her friend's house. It was one of those "all my friends are going to be there" slumber parties. I knew Dawn would be disappointed, but I figured it would give me an evening with my sister, and since we had the rest of the week it would be fine. It was only one night after all. I dropped Megan off at her friend Kristen's home and picked Dawn up at the airport. We went to get a bite to eat and Dawn couldn't wait until the next day to see Megan. We tried calling Megan with the idea of taking her and all of her friends for a quick ice cream.

There was no answer so we headed over to see Meg and her friends. I knocked on the door and Lisa, Kristen's mom, answered. I asked for Meg and Lisa said, "*She's not here.*" I asked about the sleepover and Lisa said "Sleepover? The girls didn't have a sleepover planned." It was clear she was surprised – and alarmed. “Dan, I don’t know where Meg is.” I immediately went over to Lizzie’s house, Megan’s other best friend. Lizzie’s mother also told me that Megan was never there, that no sleepover had been planned. Fear and panic were setting in. I frantically began calling Megan and Anne’s phones . . . no answer.

I raced to my apartment and dropped Dawn off en route to the police station. I was hoping that Megan had or would come home and that Dawn would call me before or when I reached the station. No such call came. I arrived at the station and told a Sergeant what had happened. He began calling Megan’s mother - no response. The Sergeant asked me if I knew where Anne lived. I told them at the extended stay hotel near UCF. They told me they would dispatch an officer do a drive by.

I left the station and headed over to the extended stay hotel. I asked the desk receptionist if Anne and Megan O’Shea were staying there and was told they could not divulge that information. An officer showed up and told me to wait in the lobby. He acquired my wife’s room number and was able to confirm that Megan was with her mother. I told him I wanted to speak with Megan. He returned with Megan, her eyes red and swollen. ”Why didn’t you tell me the truth about where you were going Meg?” I asked. No response.

“Do you understand how concerned I was for you? For what could have happened to you? Do you know what it was like for me when I didn’t know where you were?” She said nothing, but I could tell she understood me. She knew I wasn’t angry with her, but rather, that I was deeply hurt by her actions. Actions that I knew she had no power over.

I should have been angry at her mother, but I was so relieved that my Meg was safe that I really never had any room for anger. The only emotion I had any room for was profound sadness. My poor Meg. All I could do was hug her; I hugged her so very tight. “Stay with your Mom tonight. I just wanted to make sure you were okay Meg.”

“Goodbye Meg, I love you so very much.”

Later, it occurred to me that her mother knew Meg’s Aunt Dawn was visiting, the aunt Meg had been closest to. This was Anne’s way of alienating my sister from Meg too – the alienator cutting the ties that bind, not just to me, but now to my family members too.

While at work the next morning, I was informed by my attorney that Anne had filed an injunction for an order of protection against me for "feeling threatened when a police officer knocked on her door." My attorney said, "This is all spiraling out of control." I was beginning to understand my lawyer, many lawyers either didn't understand about Parental Alienation or wanted to ignore its existence. The injunction appeared on a judge's desk and was immediately denied.

Spring came to an end and with it, the end of school. Megan would spend part of the summer with me and part of it with her mother in Texas. Looming on the horizon was the divorce trial in June which continued on for several days into July. The final decision came in August.

On September 1, 2011, I received a call from my attorney. I saw the number on my caller ID and knew she was going to give me the answer I had been waiting for. I had been dreading this moment for over a year. I answered and Erin said, "*You won. Megan stays in Florida.*" Erin told me she was having the order emailed to me.

"The Final Dissolution of Marriage" is what they call it. I thanked her and hung up. There was no elation, just a deep sense of relief. My relationship with Megan was safe, I could continue to be her father. I sat down, and although I was relieved, I was also so profoundly sad. I pondered the word "won." I had *won.* To this day I despise that word. Nobody had *won*, least of all Meg. Our life as a family was over, our relationships within our family forever damaged. I had my daughter, but I had not *won.*

A few days later I received an email from Megan's mother, "I'm leaving for Texas. Megan is your responsibility now." That was it. I sat stunned, reading it several times. I got up, walked into my bedroom and sat in a chair I had by the window. I sat and cried for Megan, whose mother wanted to move away.

I wasn't sad to see Anne go, knowing the 'every other week' silence would be no more, but I was worried for Megan. I wanted her to maintain a close relationship with her Mom. I signed all of us up for a website that allowed parents and children to post photos and communicate with their parents in a kind of private Facebook. Anne would be able to see photos and read about Meg's activities based on whatever Meg wanted to share. They could also private message one another anytime they logged in. After I paid for and created the account, I emailed Anne to tell her about the site and gave her the login information. Within a day her mother responded, "How dare you put my personal information on a website. Remove it immediately!" I did.

As Megan entered her sophomore year of high school without her Mom she began to change a great deal. While it was easier for me as I didn't have to say goodbye to her every other week, it was not easier for Megan. She no longer involved herself in any extracurricular activities. She spent most evenings alone in her bedroom. The extra room we made for entertaining her friends sat empty. She stopped inviting her friends over, opting to go to their homes instead. I couldn't "read" these signs, just like I couldn't force her to do the things I knew she had once enjoyed so much. I couldn't tell if it was just a girl wanting to assert her independence or a girl still heavily influenced by her mother.

In late fall, I received Megan's first report card and to my shock it was filled with D's and F's. I was subscribed to Hagerty High School's student account, an area for both students and parents to track grades, school assignments, and quiz/test schedules. I logged in on a regular basis, and there was nothing that indicated she was doing so poorly. I immediately called her counselor and set up a meeting between me, Megan, the counselor and most of Megan's teachers. I was informed at the meeting by some of the teachers that Megan wasn't doing poorly in quizzes and tests, she just wasn't turning assignments in. I asked the teachers why this wasn't noted in the students' account. They informed me that not all of the teachers use or update the site on a regular basis. I made a plan with Meg's teachers to be in contact with them on a weekly basis.

When Megan and I got home I grounded her. She wasn't allowed to hang out with her friends, and I took away her cellphone texting plan until she improved her grades. The next day after I had returned home from work, Megan was in the living room while I was in my bedroom changing clothes. She came in and said there was someone at the door who wanted to see me. I went and opened the apartment door to a police officer. He said a call had come into the station concerning the treatment of my daughter. I asked him what the complaint was and he said, "A lady called and said you had cut off your daughter's phone communication."

I replied, "My daughter's grades were going down because she wasn't doing her assignments so I have removed texting from her cell phone. As for voice, I informed the officer I can still call her, she can still call me, she can still call her mother, and her mother can still call her and speak with her. She is not going to text friends if she isn't going to turn in school assignments." The officer replied, "I have a daughter and I'd do the same." I asked him who called in the complaint and he said, "Someone named Anne out in Texas." Before the officer left he said he would inform the station that it was a meritless complaint. He was also going to recommend that in the future they take complaints from Anne with caution before sending a unit out. I was beginning to learn that Parental Alienation also abuses government systems too.

Thanksgiving came and I took Meg to the airport for her visit to Texas and her mom.

"*Goodbye Meg, I love you very much.*"

Meg returned from Thanksgiving and the silence was filled with distance and a kind of disdain. I began dreading her visits to her mom in a new way. As if the silent treatment I would endure when she was in her Mom's care wasn't hard enough.

I went to pick Megan up from her friend's house the night before she was leaving for Texas over Christmas break. Lisa, her friend's mother, answered the door and Meg came down with the other girls she had been with. As she was beginning to say goodbye to them she turned and asked me to leave. I thought it was strange how she had asked, and how the other girls looked at me. Normally she says goodbye and we leave. Flustered and not wanting to rock the boat I left the house and stood outside waiting for Megan. We went home, finished packing, and I drove her to the airport the next day.

"*Goodbye Meg, I love you very much.*"

Two weeks later Megan was due back in Florida, and more importantly, she was due back in school. Anne informed me she would be returning a week later. No explanation - just the flight information. It was clear to me that this was the plan all along. After all that had transpired in the past year, I was well aware of the secrets that Meg was forced to keep from me. I realized she was being taught that I was not a person worthy of trust or respect. It occurred to me that she wanted a private good-bye with her friends to keep her travel dates from me.

About a week after Meg returned from Christmas break Anne struck again. I was sitting at my desk at work when I received a call from Florida's Department of Children and Family Services (DCF). I was told by the DCF agent that a complaint had been filed against me. I asked who and they said they could not tell me, it was against policy and regulations to "protect" the child and the complainant.

My co-workers were looking at me, clearly overhearing my side of the phone conversation. I was told that I would have to meet with a DCF agent and my daughter immediately. When I asked where Megan was, the agent informed me that she would be at our apartment waiting with DCF. I found out later that DCF had pulled Megan out of class in front of all of her schoolmates.

I arrived at our apartment fifteen minutes after the call to discover Megan and a DCF agent standing outside of our door. As we walked into the apartment I asked, "What is the complaint about?" She said that there was a complaint filed alleging that Megan was living in a filthy apartment and had nothing to eat.

It couldn't be. My days off from work were Sundays and Wednesdays. Every Wednesday after I took Meg to school I returned home, started the wash, and cleaned the entire apartment. It was the perfect day to do it, not Sundays, just in case Meg and I were doing something, but Wednesdays when Megan would be at school. This was a Thursday when DCF came, so the grocery shopping and cleaning had been done the day before. Not only that, I had spent several hours specifically cleaning Megan's room.

Meg and I sat on the sofa as the agent went from room to room. I wondered what Megan was thinking and feeling. I sat in silent shock. The agent witnessed beds carefully made, dressers and end-tables clean, bathroom sinks and countertops sparkling, carpets throughout vacuumed, a refrigerator so full that there wasn't room for one more item. The DCF agent closed the refrigerator door and walked over near the entrance of the apartment. She then took several steps back in and looked around, saying, almost to herself, "This is really a wonderful place." I learned later it was Megan's mother who called DCF.

After that incident, I went to sleep many nights with demons haunting me. They weren't after me . . . they were after Meg. As I tried to sleep there were so many nights where I just could not silence my mind. I could only think of what Megan must think when her own mother says there is "no food" and that she lives in "a dirty apartment." I pictured her pulled out of class in front of her friends and classmates. I felt her embarrassment and pain. I worried when and what the next "hit" would be. I lived in this constant state of worry.

Sadly, my state of worry was justified. Over the past year my employer had learned of my fight to keep Megan, but this call from DCF heightened that struggle . . . and awareness. A few days after the call that caused me to leave work abruptly, my general manager called me into his office. He began to question my "focus." "Surely all of this must distract from your job."

This was the same manager that had presented me with a "Ray Lewis" signed jersey from my favorite team, the Baltimore Ravens, while announcing in a manager's meeting, "If it hadn't been for Dan O'Shea, I'm not so sure this dealership would have survived." As a result of a system that I implemented in the internet department - a business development center called BDC - we went from struggling to keep up with 300 to 400 inquiries per month to efficiently handling over 10,000 leads per month. The end-result of that conversation was the beginning of responsibilities being removed from my internet department, cuts of department staff, and finally, the very real possibility of cuts to my pay - and with it the fear of being unable to support Meg and my other obligations. It was also the beginning of another huge battle.

When I started working for the dealership in 2009 I was making $4000 per month ($500 of that was commission). By 2011 my commission rose to $4500 per month! I was making more money than I ever had in my life. I should have been on easy street (I should have been enjoying this success with my wife and children). Even after taxes my take-home was around $6000. Unfortunately, between lifelong alimony of $2,000 per month and various other court-ordered expenses, my obligations were $3,000 per month. Anne was enjoying a lifestyle that we didn't have when we were married.

In all the years we were together at my highest point, I barely made over $3000 per month. I supported 6 people on that income. I remember asking my attorney "How is it a court can order payments for an amount for just one person that was just a little bit less than what we had together in our 30 years of marriage for 6 people?" Her answer? "Consider it legal blackmail for getting your daughter back."

In addition to the money I had to give Anne I had an even bigger concern. When the order was signed I asked my attorney what would happen if my commissions went down. The financial agreement counted my commission as regular income, even though my commission was not guaranteed each month. "All you have to do in that case is file a petition for income modification, it's very standard and very easy." I learned later this was far from the truth.

My general manager decided that I should take less responsibility and also less pay. It was the first hint that my ex-wife's DCF complaint and the earlier injunction attempt was having an impact on my career. Shortly after that, the general manager informed me that I would have to remove my department supervisor and a few of the BDC consultants. It became apparent that the internet responsibilities were being systematically removed to the sales floor. I began to apply to various dealerships, expecting to be removed from the internet department as rumors abounded. Both the fear of taking care of Megan and complying with paying lifetime alimony were front and center.

I searched for a job in my field as a BDC manager, (1) Because it was what I was good at and (2) Because I had to follow the law. The moment we filed divorce we all became "wards of the state," not just Megan. The family court not only determined her future, where she should live and when she would spend time with her mother or me, it also ruled over my life. I could not move to a new city with my daughter without filing a petition. I also could not quit my job without having another one. I could not take a job as a lifeguard or street sweeper unless it brought in as much income as BDC. I had to seek out a lateral position or be in contempt of court.

I found a position at another dealership, one that I was hoping would have more job security. It was still a cut in pay, but at least I didn't have the history of the DCF call attached to me. Wanting, and needing to meet my obligations as well as provide stability for Megan, I continued my search for a job that would replace my previous income. I submitted applications from as far north as South Georgia down to South Florida in the hopes of finding a BDC position.

While Megan was in Texas for the summer, I found a position in

South Georgia. I was hired by a former assistant general manager of Carl Black to rebuild their internet department and establish a BDC. I found a beautiful little place near the ocean in Fernandina Beach, Florida - only 2 hours from Oviedo. I tried to make the transition as easy as possible for Megan; I thought staying close to Oviedo to visit her friends would be a great thing for her. I also didn't think that other than her friends she would care where we lived. She was no longer involved in any after-school activities. I also hoped that the change in school would take away some of her distractions and improve her grades. Aside from that, and most importantly, this position would keep me on the right side of the law – a lateral job move.

I picked Megan up from the airport at the end of summer and told her about the move. She was devastated. I was shocked at her response. I really thought that other than her friends she had no real attachment to Oviedo. Here I was trying to do everything right and now the one thing that mattered most to me I had fallen short of: Megan's happiness. I was devastated and terrified I was going to lose her both emotionally and physically.

I dropped Meg off at her best friend's home so that she could spend a few days there while I returned to Fernandina Beach to work. I was trying to figure out what to do when a former sales manager at Carl Black contacted me. He had recently reached out to me with a job offer in Miami and was now offering me an opportunity to be the Internet Director of not just one dealership but of two more dealerships in the works as well, one in Fort Lauderdale and another in Orlando within the year. Hope arose to be situated back where Meg and I had been in Oviedo, Florida.

The following morning, I spoke with Megan's best friend's mother, Lisa, who brought up the possibility of Megan staying with them while I worked in Miami. I spoke with Megan and asked her if this was something she wanted to do. I also gave her the option to live with her mother in Texas, visiting me on all holidays and summers. In the meantime, Anne had received my petition to modify income and my motion to relocate, to which she did not respond. Nor did she respond to my email concerning Megan living with Lisa or with her in Texas.

Before making any final decisions, I called our last counselor, Robin, who had counseled both Megan and me. I filled her in and asked her what she felt would be best for Megan. Robin stated she had seen a number of children Megan's age – 16, living in stable environments away from their parents. She said they did very well as long as one or both parents maintained close contact with regular communication and visits.

Several days later Megan told me that her mother was fine with her staying with Lisa. I took the job in Miami, and prior to leaving I set Lisa up with a bank account where I would deposit weekly money for Megan's needs and expenses. Megan also had an account that I would put money in for her allowance and other incidentals. I visited Megan in Oviedo every weekend and kept in daily contact by phone and email. I was happy that she was where she wanted to be, but I missed her terribly. I was looking forward to the day I would be back in Oviedo full time.

In the middle of September (only 6 weeks into my new position), I was with my staff in the internet department when I was informed that someone had come in asking for me. I went to the showroom, and in front of the sales staff and managers, a process server served me with contempt papers from Anne for not paying alimony. I was served even though I had filed an income modification with the court. The following day I was called into the office by the general manager and asked what was going on. I told him about the filing and my divorce. Later that day I left for the weekend to visit Meg in Oviedo. When I returned to work on Monday morning, I was informed that my services were no longer required.

I went back to Orlando, jobless, consoled only by the fact that I would be near Meg. I found a room to rent and worked odd jobs (while looking for full-time employment) that allowed me to continue to support Meg. I saw her almost daily. In October, I was hired by a company in a call center. The company had the promise of moving to a more lucrative high security position in their credit card division. As I trained for the call center with the thought of a better position on the horizon, I began apartment hunting for Megan and me.

After only two weeks in my new position I was called into human resources and informed that, "someone by the name of Anne O'Shea had called inquiring about you." Again, I had to explain the conflict between my ex-wife and me. I racked my brain trying to figure out how Anne would have been able to find out where I was working. Never mind trying to figure why she would not want to keep me working, asking myself, "how did she think I would be able to pay her alimony if I didn't have a job?" It finally occurred to me that the only way Anne could have found out where I was led back to Megan. I had a security badge that hung from the car mirror. Megan obviously saw it when I took her to and from school. That phone call destroyed any hope of moving to a high security position and with it any possibility of a home for Meg and me. I kept my job at the call center while trying to find another BDC position, or any other job that would allow me to have a home with Meg.

By early December of 2012, I could no longer afford the room I rented. All of my money was now being sent to Lisa's and Meg's accounts. I took an inflatable mattress I had in storage and put it in my SUV. That night, after dropping Megan off at Lisa's home, I parked in a secluded spot and laid in the back. For the first time in my life, I was homeless.

As I laid there, I saw Christmas lights far in the distance; my thoughts of Meg, being with Lisa's family, that she was safe and sound . . . and she at least had a Christmas tree and decorations this Christmas season as I drifted to sleep.

A couple of weeks later I received a call from a law firm in South Florida. They were looking for someone to help them build an internet application for foreclosures. I interviewed for the position and was hired. My salary was far below what I needed to pay for the original ordered lifetime alimony, but it would be enough to support Megan. I started with the law firm in the first week of January and continued to file hundreds of applications, focusing on the Orlando area, hoping to find employment closer to Meg.

Very little time had passed when a call came into my office that someone wanted to see me. I went to the front of the office and was served with contempt papers, again. A day or two later, my boss informed me that I would no longer be on salary. I would only be receiving "commission." Given the fact that the internet application I was building had not yet been completed, this meant I would have to live with no income until the application was finished.

Luckily, a friend in Fort Lauderdale knew of a brokerage company that wanted to hire a consultant for their internet marketing. I began working with them in March.

In the middle of April, a new judge was assigned to our case, Judge

Linda Schoonover. I received an email from the court in Seminole County for a hearing. By law, a twenty-day notification is required; I only received one day's notice. As I lived 3 hours away from Seminole County, I had less than 24 hours to prepare for the hearing, where I was to present my petition to modify income along with my response to Anne's contempt motions.

I entered the courtroom and the proceedings began. Judge Schoonover refused my request to hear my petition to modify income, giving no reason for her decision. Instead she focused on Anne's contempt motion. Jean was allowed to testify to alleged "abuse" she never saw, and when I objected to the hearsay, the bailiff told me to be quiet. I respectfully requested again that the judge hear my petition to modify income, and was denied.

Judge Schoonover ordered Megan to be picked up at Cocoa Beach where she was spending the day with friends, and returned to the court. In chambers Meg told the judge that she did not want to live with me in South Florida or her mother in Texas. Judge Schoonover ordered Megan to remain with her best friend's family until a psychological evaluation was completed. I was held in contempt and ordered to report to the county jail if I did not pay $1,000 to my ex-wife within forty-eight hours. At that point, the monthly alimony I owed had risen to almost $50,000, despite paying periodically what I could.

I was in the courthouse lobby when I saw Meg. I went up to her and told her how proud of her I was. "I'm proud of you for speaking up . . . not for me, not for your mother, but for you."

"*Goodbye Meg, I love you very much.*"

I drove back to Fort Lauderdale and within two days I paid the $1,000 to Megan's mother. I was left with nothing. I had no money to make my car payment, my rent, or to give to Lisa. Shortly after, my car was repossessed and I lost my studio apartment I acquired several months before. I received a hand-written court order within a week and was stunned. Judge Schoonover asserted that I had "kept the child support the mother was sending for Megan." There was no testimony ever to that effect. If there had been, I would have easily testified and presented bank statements that proved I was depositing money, including Anne's support to Meg into an account on a weekly basis.

And the hits just kept on coming as Anne petitioned to have Meg in Texas. Her petition met none of the requirements set forth under Florida law . . . not one.

During and after the divorce process, Megan and I participated in counseling, both separately and together. Rather than allowing Megan to be evaluated by a counselor who knew her well, the judge ordered that we, Anne, Meg and I, would be evaluated by a new court appointed counselor. A complete stranger that had no clue as to the history of repeated alienation by Anne. Prior to the interviews we were all required to submit detailed information regarding our positions and concerns. In the information I gave to the counselor, I included as many details as I could regarding Anne's repeated attempts to alienate Megan from me. Everything from the DCF call to her preventing contact when Meg was in her "care."

In May, Judge Schoonover held another hearing, and in ten short minutes, the future of my relationship with Megan was determined for the rest of our lives. The court-appointed counselor, in his "recommendation" (he spoke with each of us individually for 30 minutes) stated that "Megan should be relocated to Texas and that both parents agreed." A lie. Judge Schoonover agreed with the recommendation and Megan was ordered to go to Texas. I asked Judge Schoonover about child sharing. She stated that there would be none. No reason for her answer. None.

How could a judge take a child away from her dad and her and give to a mother who has done everything under the sun to damage her child's relationship with her father? A mother who violated the laws governing child custody at every turn? Everything from cutting off communication to not supplying the address of where my daughter was living, not to mention discussing the details of every legal filing with Meg. How could a judge order our whole family to be evaluated in 90-minutes and use that as a basis to determine the rest of our daughter's life?

Here is just one of the laws on the books that should have protected my relationship with Meg:

> Florida Family Law:
>
> 61.13 Support of children; parenting and

time-sharing; powers of court. -

1. It is the public policy of this state that each minor child has frequent and continuing contact with both parents after the parents separate or the marriage of the parties is dissolved to encourage parents to share the rights and responsibilities, and joys of childrearing. There is no presumption for or against the father or mother of the child or for or against any specific time- sharing schedule when creating or modifying the parenting plan of the child.
2. The court *shall* order that the parental responsibility for a minor child be shared by both parents unless the court finds that shared parental responsibility would be detrimental to the child.

In legal terms, "may" and "shall" are critically important. "May" means a court has discretion. "Shall" means it should be. In other words, the law in my case states, "Megan shall be shared by both parents unless the court finds that shared parental responsibility would be detrimental to Megan." How could there be any detriment? The same court ruled Megan would continue to live in the home of her best friend's family. There was no finding, just an order that I would have no shared time.

As if losing Meg wasn't enough, Judge Schoonover was far from done with me. I would still be required to pay $2,000 in alimony plus $480 in child support per month. Never mind that I was only earning $2,400 per month. The judge stated that a hearing would be held prior to the end of summer to make a final determination. No such hearing was ever called or held.

This is the last email I received from Meg after I texted her after the hearing:

Sent: Thursday, May 9, 2013 8:53 AM
To: Dan

> Subject: Text
>
> I don't feel like talking on the phone, I already talked to mom yesterday and told her I need to live with her in Texas, my anxiety has gotten to like how it was in third grade and I can't finish school I need to go to a doctor or something. She's going to fly in some time this weekend and were leaving sometime next week. I love you and ill call you later when I feel better
>
> Sent from my iPhone

Three or four days later, the day before Megan was set to leave for Texas, she called me asking if I would put some money in her bank account for her trip. I said yes, as I had always done, "I will Megan. I don't want to lose you Meg," my voice breaking. She said "you won't."

"*Goodbye Meg, I love you very much.*"

She said, "*I love you too.*" Those were her final words to me.

I tried calling and emailing Meg hundreds of times in the next several months, only to be met with deafening silence. After the second month, as I was paying Meg's phone bill I noticed that her normal hundred phone calls each month had reduced to just six. I could only believe that they had given Megan a new phone and didn't inform me.

With one decision made in ten minutes, Meg was taken from me . . . and her aunts, her uncles, her cousins . . . everyone on her father's side. One decision by one person. Her future was forever altered. Our futures were forever altered. I was no longer a father. I was defeated, I was deflated; I was nothing. The position of "father," "dad" usurped forever.

Some of my final emails to Meg:

> From: Dan
> Sent: Friday, May 31, 2013 6:50 AM
> To: Megan

Subject: Hope Your Ok

I've tried calling many times and haven't heard back. Are you mad at me? Have no idea why unless its because you had to go. I tried everything Meg but just can't find a good job in this economy.

Also looked at phone records. No calls out or in to any of your Florida friends, not even your best friends.

Just let me know your ok. No matter how long, you can always call me. Until then, I'll always wait for your call.
I love you so much.

Dad

Sent from my iPhone

From: Dan
Sent: Friday, May 31, 2013 12:12 PM
To: Megan
Subject: I Miss You

I miss you terribly Meg. Love you always.

Dad

From: Dan
Sent: Wednesday, June 5, 2013 11:10 PM
To: Megan
Subject: Where are you?

Meg,
I keep trying to call you. Your voicemail box is full. Please call me.

I love you.

Dad

From: Dan
Sent: Thursday, June 20, 2013 8:30 AM
To: Megan
Subject: Happy Birthday

Happy Birthday Meg.

I miss and love you very much.

Dad

From: Dan
Sent: Monday, July 15, 2013 9:33 PM
To: Megan
Subject: Miss You

I miss you Meg.

Always love you.

Dad

From: Dan
Sent: Wednesday, July 24, 2013 2:06 PM
To: Megan
Subject: Miss You

Miss and love you Meg.

Please call me.

Dad

From: Dan
Sent: Wednesday, July 31, 2013 9:32 AM
To: Megan
Subject: MY

I do miss you terribly.

Dad

From: Dan
Sent: Thursday, August 8, 2013 11:11 AM
To: Megan
Subject: Miss and Love You

I miss and love you Meg.

From: Dan O'Shea
Sent: Wednesday, August 14, 2013 5:42 PM
To: Megan
Subject: Miss You

I miss you Meg.

I hope you are ok and doing well. You are an amazing person. Reach the goals with the gifts you were born with.

I love and miss you terribly.

Dad

From: Dan
Sent: Saturday, August 24, 2013 12:05 AM
To: Megan
Subject: Always

Always think of you, miss you and love you.

I hope you're doing well.

Dad

From: Dan
Sent: Monday, August 26, 2013 8:49 PM
To: Megan
Subject: Love You

"You have been the most amazing girl I have ever known. And you're growing up and you're still amazing me. You are an incredible person. I love you very much. Take care."

I love and miss you very much.

Dad

From: Dan
Sent: Saturday, September 7, 2013 10:26 AM
To: Megan
Subject: No One

No one in your lifetime could ever love you more than I have, do or will.

I love and miss you.

Dad

Below is my last message, the last words I sent to Meg:

From: Dan
Sent: Friday, September 13, 2013 7:43 PM
To: Megan
Subject: Will Always

Will always love you.

Chapter 12

All That Remains –
Through the Pained-Glass Window of Twitter

"What has become of our Little Boy Blue,
Since he kissed them and put them there."

As the alienation of my daughter began, I'd say goodbye every other Monday morning, dropping her off at school, knowing I most likely wouldn't hear from her for a week. In those silent weeks I'd spend most nights at the corner pub.

I would take a seat in a dark corner of the pub where I could be alone in the shadows. Thinking of all four of my children, and especially of Meg, the last one who didn't have the choice to leave like the others did.

After Megan was taken away the last time and I never saw or heard from her again, there was little reason to go to the nearby pub and wait until it was time to pick her up.

Even so, one day out of habit I went to the pub. Taking my corner booth in the shadows I began my search and found Megan on Twitter.

And so it began.

A new reason to go to that outside corner seat of the pub once or twice a week: it was there that I could meet with Meg again.

With my face pressed up against the Twitter window hoping to somehow see more . . . never daring to "follow" her, out of the fear and knowledge that her mother would block me the way she had with Meg's Facebook profile.

On a Saturday, June 28, 2015 at 4:38 p.m., Meg posted:

> "If you have a good relationship with
> your father, you are incredibly lucky."

My daughter's Twitter post spoke volumes of the conflicted alienated child.

It was on Twitter that I was able to see her buy her first car. I saw her hired for her first job as a hostess at a restaurant. I saw that she became an aunt for the first time, her sister giving birth to a baby girl. It was here on Twitter that I found out I was a grandfather through her sister.

Sometimes the posts were like small talk, as a parent-child do when together. Then there were posts revealing that a new life event had occurred.

It was my way to visit with her, as we did the night when she was the *apple of my eye.*

In my mind we sat, talked of those things of little importance, smiled, and just profoundly enjoyed the moment of being together.

Several times a week even now, the schedule is set, and there, at that same spot at the corner pub, we meet again.

Through the pained-glass window of Twitter.

PART III - ALIENATION & ESTRANGEMENT

Chapter 13

Parental Alienation Syndrome (PAS)

At this point you may be asking, despite all that Anne did to alienate me from my Megan, how did she manage to "win" in the end? One I still ask myself even though in some ways I know the answer.

For starters, he - or in this case, she - with more money wins. Anne had unlimited funds to fight with, and with more money comes better lawyers. Add to that ignorance. Until the courts recognize PAS and hold the perpetrators responsible, our children will continue to be emotionally abused and taken from their families.

Why won't the courts recognize Parental Alienation Syndrome? Because organizations such as the American Psychiatric Association do not recognize Parental Alienation Syndrome. This lack of recognition means that when our children are evaluated, PAS is not on the landscape of what a court-appointed therapist would be looking for. Furthermore, the counselors evaluating the children and parents that are involved in the divorce process are not all equally degreed, there is no set standard. Even if PAS was recognized, the "professionals" are not all trained equally.

Beyond that, another question comes into play: “How can a counselor adequately evaluate the parents and child enough in 30 minutes to make a recommendation that affects the rest of their lives?” And another question: “When will the courts and psychological community recognize and protect families from Parental Alienation Syndrome?”

The destruction, trauma and sorrow of Parental Alienation Syndrome has far reaching effects, with lasting detriments to the children, parents and families involved. While the American Psychological Association ignores PAS because of their belief that it “is not a syndrome,” millions of parents and families suffer the symptoms that shouts that it “is.” These symptoms are not hard to see and are consistent with PAS.

I. The Destruction Caused by Parental Alienation Syndrome

When my experience with Parental Alienation Syndrome began, little did I know of the full force and weight that would come from the alienator and her enablers. I reeled from her constant assaults, unable to comprehend her actions after a lifetime of devotion and duty to her and our children. The very worst was seeing firsthand the destruction of our child's life as she had known it, the child I loved, we loved. I myself have witnessed and felt extensive and damaging experiences of Parental Alienation, but I am sure there are even more that others who are victims of PAS have endured.

a. *The Beginning of PAS - Everything you say and do will be used against you.*

Early on, before I understood the actions of an alienator and enablers, I didn't know how my desperate struggles and actions in reacting to the alienator would be used against me. If there is one thing I would hope a person who is just beginning to experience Parental Alienation Syndrome is how to respond. Looking at the twenty-twenty vision retroactively back, the beginning for me was the nightly hours Megan's mother laid with her in her room, the door closed. I soon learned the main topic was where they would live without me, as Megan's mother asked her where she would want to live, in Florida or back in South Carolina.

The parent left out in such plans without opinion or say over their child's life brings about desperate words or actions. I can remember mine. I emailed in panic to Megan's mother, "There is nothing redemptive left." My words and reaction derived from the catastrophic fear of losing Megan, and with it, our life together and raising our four children, together. But her enablers didn't experience the nightly closed-door visits between a parent and child planning their separation from the other parent. Instead, the mere words I emailed were used against me.

Or in another example early on, when Megan was taken to Texas the first time without my knowledge, I emailed Anne and pleaded with her to let us work it out, she and I. She emailed back totally rejecting my plea. I reacted and changed my Facebook profile to "single." The purpose to let her see what she was doing. Again, this was used against me. My point here is that a victim of PAS early on can't react! If I only knew then what the psychiatric community and legal professionals won't advise victims of PAS of – don't react, in anger or words.

I would have sought the aid of those who have experienced PAS on social media and the few psychologists and legal professionals experienced in PAS. I just didn't know it at the time, but no matter how right a victim of PAS is in words or actions, momentary reactions of the realization of the taking of one's child by the actions of another parent fuels the fire of the enabler for the alienator.

b. *The Past - The history of who you were will be re-written.*

In my case, I had two people in a court of law attempt to portray me as an abuser, including my ex-wife's sister Jean who saw me three times for less than an hour each in ten years. False accusations, false testimony. Even those who knew you best will forget who you are. My other children took their mother's side under the pressure of her entire half of the family.

c. *The relationship you have as the Mother or Father of your child will never be the same.*

When Megan was first taken to Texas, I was not allowed to speak with her for the most part, and when I did, there was no more "small talk" as we once had. Children are open books and speak their minds freely. That was no more, the book was closed. When I called her I had to ask the questions, I was never asked one. All of the times we had shared before, doing things together, it was all gone. When Meg returned, I asked her if she wanted to take a cooking class or get involved in something together. There was no longer any interest. I understood there were voices "on the other side" always talking to her.

d. *Your child will change and won't be as you knew her or him.*

The happy go-lucky fourteen-year-old girl I knew, always smiling, talking and chatting about everything and nothing, was gone. The disparaging voice of the alienator brought turmoil to the child, in harsh conflict with their own memories of love and devotion with the alienated parent. The child is forever changed by the mentally abusive trauma and destruction of Parental Alienation.

e. *Your child will be caught in the middle.*

While I kept silent, her mother fed her any and all of the information that she possibly could. Anne was asked in court "How much were you discussing this with your child?" "Everything," her mother answered. Meg was being told "everything" from one perspective, and there was nothing I could have done. I followed the law and we all lost . . . some of us more than others, even my other children. To cite one example, when I finally moved out of our house I left behind some marital property for Anne to keep if she so chose. I sent her an email, and instead of asking me for the keys or asking one of my sisters, she went through our son Ryan. By doing this, she made it appear that I was trying to keep her from going into the home.

She also kept Meg caught in the middle. Filing a DCF report, calling the police, Megan lying about the sleepover . . . the list goes on and on. These became the constant messages to Megan that instructed her to no longer hold me in esteem, no longer trust me, no longer respect or value her Dad. The alienator ignores the fact that our daughter is two halves - one me and the other her mother. How could my little Meg grow up loving herself when half of her is "bad?"

f. *Your child's events and activities will be lost.*

The talent shows, music concerts, and other school performances will be missed. You simply will not be informed or invited. For the child, it becomes a matter of having to choose. The alienator says, "If your Dad (or Mom) goes, I'm not going." PAS lays the guilt trip on the child.

g. *Respect as Mom or Dad will be lost.*

I've read experience after experience of the alienated parent who was sworn at by their children, or who lost the highest title of respect they could hold as a parent as their children no longer called them "Mom" or "Dad" but by their first name. When the alienator shows a child that they can treat the other parent with such disrespect, the natural respect of a child to a parent is lost forever. My experiences herein reflect the respect of "Dad" lost.

h. *There will be a separation from family and friends you knew.*

In several ways; family members on the alienator's side will become his or her enabler. Years of friendship and truth will be exchanged simply to support or pacify the alienator. My ex-wife met and roomed with a college friend named Sue that became a life-long friend. Before and after our marriage we both became good friends with Sue and her husband Jared. We visited them many times in New Jersey and they visited us in Maryland. We even vacationed with them on several occasions. Remarkably, when Meg was taken to Texas and I spoke with Jared, he kept wanting to talk about "abuse" and how it occurred with one of his employee's. I finally asked him, "Jared, in all the times we were together, give me an example of how you ever saw me abuse Anne?" He couldn't, his silence screamed at me. His wife Sue, my ex-wife's best friend, sent me an email shortly after, "You may win the war, but you'll lose Anne and Megan." The enabler spoke and I never heard from these "dear friends" again.

Other friends, co-workers and acquaintances won't understand, and because of that, will keep a distance from you that you never knew before. One family member, after I related some of the things my ex-wife did, asked, "Why would she do such things?" Many don't understand the vengeance and cruelty of Parental Alienation.

There was also the time when I was sitting outside at the corner pub among friends and some were asking about Megan and the issues of alienation. One woman looked over and said, "Well, you must have done something!" There was no mortal sin committed under God, there was no crime committed under the law. Where does the judgment of earthly separation from one's child come from? The natural right of a child to know her mother or father. Until Parental Alienation is recognized, the alienated parent will wear a scarlet letter.

i. *There will be a scorched earth.*

This began at the outset of my alienation, when my ex-wife and her sister removed half of our marital property and took, as my sister described, "everything I ever loved." It continued when they established a bank account together and transferred the funds from our marital account, and when Anne refused to communicate with me, despite all of the shared decisions that had to be made. Decisions that changed everything. From homes to accounts to our pension. Everything. Eventually because the alienator will agree to nothing in family court, family funds are depleted to the legal professionals and for some, the last possession in life – the inalienable right to Life, Liberty, and the Pursuit of Happiness – is denied and replaced by lifetime servitude or even prison.

There was a time before alienation, when we were married and while I worked, that our children's mother made sure their schoolwork was completed and that the grades were a B or higher. No more. With Parental Alienation, Megan's grades deteriorated, even when her mother was in Florida. I was the one who had to call school counselors and arrange parent-teacher meetings. To hell with her education, to hell with her grades - it was if her mother was saying, "In this manner I can show the court that Megan isn't doing well and why she needs to go to Texas," not caring that these grades would follow her in any attempt for college. Scorched earth.

Another example was our pension. I had, by working for United Parcel Service, earned a pension through Teamsters Union Local 639. As we were going through our initial separation, I was eligible to receive benefits from a choice of five different options, one of which had to be chosen yet could never be changed. The two best options were either 1 - an $1,800 per month benefit (that she would continue to receive half if I passed away,) or 2 - a $2,700 per month benefit (she would not receive anything after I passed away.) I was not required to exercise the first option, but for the second option or any other I was required to have her signature too. I asked my wife (at the time) if she would agree to option two and we would have an attorney prepare a legal document requiring me to maintain a life insurance policy so she would receive a lump sum in the event of my death. She refused and so I put the application on hold.

As her legal bills were paid by her family, my legal bills were adding up while my funds were drying up. I finally exercised option 1 after six months, limiting our monthly pension to $1,800 per month. I received a

$9,000 lump sum check for the unpaid prior months during the application process and paid my legal bills. But henceforth and forever until death, our pension was limited to $1,800 per month and divided between us, not $2,700. Scorched earth.

j. Silence, secrets and whispers will abound.

Out of all of my ex-wife's family, her brothers and sisters Chris, Greg, Paul, Katie and David, our good friends, and three of our four children, none came to testify of any perceived "abuse." They knew the truth and they weren't going to lie on the stand. So what was it that I, the alienated, did to receive a lifetime conviction of never having or seeing Meg again? I was never told. I was never informed. Not one of them ever called and asked me, "Dan, did you do this or do that?" Or, "I was told that you did this or that, tell me why you did it?" Not once.

During the final months Megan was with me, I was informed that she had a second phone, given to her by her mother and kept secret from me. Shortly thereafter I learned that communications were made between the court and my ex-wife that I was never informed of, even to this day.

While the signs and experiences of Parental Alienation were real, and most by hard facts, it is hard to believe that they were not permissible for testimony at any subsequent hearing held in all of the contempt charges filed by Megan's mother. At the first contempt hearing when Jean started to testify to "abuse," I objected. The court officer approached me and informed me that I was to remain silent to the objection that it was hearsay. The judge told me to keep my testimony only with respect to "the child." Yet Jean was able to allege abuse.

All of those signs - signs of PAS that I included in my interview with the court appointed counselor - were ignored. In that final ten-minute hearing, none of my concerns or evidence was discussed, and my attempts to discuss them were denied.

Even without recognizing PAS, the fact remained that Anne was in direct violation of more than half of the laws governing custody in the state of Florida. This alone should have been grounds for Megan remaining in my care, or at least where she was, while I was getting re-established. The laws in place were clear, as they are in all states.

Family law in Florida, as in all states, dictates that there are twenty major points that determine whether a child may be relocated elsewhere, and either remain or be removed from their current environment, with the best interest of the child being the primary consideration. Furthermore, such changes will not be made without a thorough evaluation of all factors affecting the welfare, interests, and circumstances of the minor child and family, including, but not limited to:

> 61.13 Support of children; parenting and time-sharing; powers of court.—
>
> (3) For purposes of establishing or *modifying parental responsibility and creating, developing, approving, or modifying a parenting plan, including a time-sharing schedule, which governs each parent's relationship with his or her minor child* and the relationship between each parent with regard to his or her minor child, the best interest of the child shall be the primary consideration. A determination of parental responsibility, a parenting plan, or a time-sharing schedule may not be modified without a showing of a substantial, material, and unanticipated change in circumstances and a determination that the modification is in the best interests of the child. *Determination of the best interests of the child shall be made by evaluating all of the factors* affecting the welfare and interests of the particular minor child and the circumstances of that family, including, but not limited to:
>
> (a) The demonstrated capacity and disposition of each parent to facilitate and encourage a close and

continuing parent-child relationship, to honor the time-sharing schedule, and to be reasonable when changes are required.

(b) The anticipated division of parental responsibilities after the litigation, including the extent to which parental responsibilities will be delegated to third parties.

(c) The demonstrated capacity and disposition of each parent to determine, consider, and act upon the needs of the child as opposed to the needs or desires of the parent.

(d) The length of time the child has lived in a stable, satisfactory environment and the desirability of maintaining continuity.

(e) The geographic viability of the parenting plan, with special attention paid to the needs of school-age children and the amount of time to be spent traveling to effectuate the parenting plan. This factor does not create a presumption for or against relocation of either parent with a child.

(f) The moral fitness of the parents.

(g) The mental and physical health of the parents.

(h) The home, school, and community record of the child.

(i) The reasonable preference of the child, if the court deems the child to be of sufficient intelligence, understanding, and experience to express a preference.

(j) The demonstrated knowledge, capacity, and disposition of each parent to be informed of the circumstances of the minor child, including, but not limited to, the child's friends, teachers, medical care providers, daily activities, and favorite things.

(k) The demonstrated capacity and disposition of each parent to provide a consistent routine for the child, such as discipline, and daily schedules for homework, meals, and bedtime.

(l) The demonstrated capacity of each parent to communicate with and keep the other parent informed of issues and activities regarding the minor child, and the willingness of each parent to adopt a unified front on all major issues when dealing with the child.

(m) Evidence of domestic violence, sexual violence, child abuse, child abandonment, or child neglect, regardless of whether a prior or pending action relating to those issues has been brought. If the court accepts evidence of prior or pending actions regarding domestic violence, sexual violence, child abuse, child abandonment, or child neglect, the court must specifically acknowledge in writing that such evidence was considered when evaluating the best interests of the child.

(n) Evidence that either parent has knowingly provided false information to the court regarding any prior or pending action regarding domestic violence, sexual violence, child abuse, child abandonment, or child neglect.

(o) The particular parenting tasks customarily performed by each parent and the division of parental responsibilities before the institution of litigation and during the pending litigation, including the extent to which parenting responsibilities were undertaken by third parties.

(p) The demonstrated capacity and disposition of each parent to participate and be involved in the child's school and extracurricular activities.

(q) The demonstrated capacity and disposition of each parent to maintain an environment for the child which is free from substance abuse.

(r) The capacity and disposition of each parent to protect the child from the ongoing litigation as demonstrated by not discussing the litigation with the child, not sharing documents or electronic media related to the litigation with the child, and refraining from disparaging comments about the other parent to the child.

(s) The developmental stages and needs of the child and the demonstrated capacity and disposition of each parent to meet the child's developmental needs.

(t) Any other factor that is relevant to the determination of a specific parenting plan, including the time-sharing schedule.

In my case, my ex-wife never filed a relocation motion, the court never addressed the twenty points under law. Megan was handed over to her mother and taken to Texas, and I never heard from her again.

II. The Trauma of Parental Alienation Syndrome

When the separation began I told Megan, "It's not your fault, you did nothing wrong." As an alienated parent, neither did I – and neither did you if you are alienated from your own children. The experiences you felt when the alienation began and continued are a common thread; as the alienated parent, you did nothing wrong to deserve being condemned to earthly isolation from your child, or the feelings and thoughts that come to you during the day . . . and at night. You did nothing to deserve the trauma you will incessantly endure as the alienated parent.

a. *The feeling of abandonment - your walk is now alone.*

When your child is taken and your spouse leaves, you will feel abandoned, especially when it leads to the isolation of your child. You as a mom or dad will feel as though you were replaced, not just removed as a spouse, but as the mother or father of your children. Your title and your identity stripped. You may have family that stands behind you – I was lucky to have the support of my family – but nothing will ever fill the void that Parental Alienation creates.

b. *The harsh reality of the concept of "me" instead of "we."*

My brother Don had experienced divorce with his first wife Maria, a wonderful woman that I have to include here. While they as man and wife had their differences, not once did she or my brother ever attempt to isolate or alienate the other from their children Ross and Kyle. My sisters, and especially my Mom, loved Maria for the sacrifices she made so that they would always know both their Mom . . . and Dad. I recalled my Mom crying in relief when Maria said she would not move away. We, I, love Maria as a sister. Donnie could see how distraught I was over Megan when my own divorce started and said to me, "Danny, you better take care of yourself first, because if you don't, you won't be there to take care of Megan."

For years all I thought of was my wife and my children. It was an extremely difficult change to think of myself first. It was one of the most difficult experiences of my life, and I am certain that without my sisters' help moving and settling into the new apartment I got for Megan and myself, it would not have been possible.

c. *Outlets are hard to find.*

Because Parental Alienation remains hidden from the public's awareness, it is difficult for the alienated parent to find the means to deal with the isolation and alienation of their child. Extraordinarily, even today, the American Psychiatric Association's Diagnostic and Statistical Manual of Mental Disorders (DSM-V) does not recognize Parental Alienation as an "official disorder," despite the fact that it affects so many. While it has been documented since the 1980's, politics rule in favor of a child isolated from a parent, and because of this, Parental Alienation remains as a silent cancer, permeating the system, spreading its poison. As long as that prevails, any outlets to find comfort, understanding and help remain elusive. Counseling sessions, divorce groups, and court hearings seldom if ever recognize Parental Alienation.

There was no outlet for me and there is little for alienated parents today. I have found recently that within social media and Facebook there is an extremely fast-growing grassroots movement of Parental Alienation awareness, noted by many new Facebook pages devoted to the subject. These groups are the first outlet for those enduring Parental Alienation to find some comfort and see that their experience is much more common than ever realized. Parents, Grandparents and families around the world are awakening to the burgeoning abuse of PAS.

d. *Fear settles in.*

For me, it wasn't that Megan would live without me at times. It was fear that Parental Alienation would succeed as it eventually did . . . leading to a lifetime separation. Even when I shared time with Megan, the constant threat of the Motion to Relocate was held over me like a sledgehammer aimed at my soul. I knew if it succeeded, all contact with Megan would be lost. Ironically, my ex-wife's motion was denied at first by the court, yet several years later after the two-year struggle with PAS, a court allowed Megan to relocate without even the required filing of a motion.

e. *The alienation and isolation is a deep depression.*

For almost thirty years, I made little friends. I left home for work each morning at 7:30 a.m. and returned between 7 p.m. and 9 p.m. on most nights. My family was my life. I had no time for anyone else. I didn't want to make time for anyone else. My wife and my children were everything to me. They were my existence. When my wife took Megan, there was nothing to fill the void. The cruel act had a purpose, and Megan's mother knew it. The act of love for almost thirty years was used against me. As she told my sisters when she took Megan, "He has no friends." Of course I didn't, I had worked so hard and so much for my family, of course all of my free time went to being with them. They were my world and my world was shattered by PAS.

f. *Your purpose-filled life is gone.*

When my child was taken, my purpose was taken. Everything I did for over 30 years was for my family, and now it was all gone.

g. *The foundation of your belief system is shaken to the core.*

I was a spiritual person. I believed in God and his scriptures. I married under those precepts, believing if I honored God, my wife, and my children and put them first, that no harm would come to my family. Unfortunately, my wife's religious beliefs left her with a Pollyanna vision of a perfect husband that I could not compete with. I was not a perfect human being, I was not a perfect dad, but I did the best that I could, as my Dad had done before me. Even if you are not religious, a loving parent has an innate desire and responsibility to care and love their child. Even this is shaken to the core by Parental Alienation.

h. *Never-ending goodbyes, so many places, so many people.*

When a child is taken, the alienated parent can't resolve the goodbyes. Each time I said goodbye to Megan it cut like a knife, knowing the silence that would ensue. Dropping her off at school and watching her walk away for a week without hearing from her. Dropping her off at the airport on a holiday knowing I would not hear from her for weeks, or for the summer where communication would be almost nonexistent. When she was away, I would pass places where we spent time together, missing her all the more. Sometimes I would catch a glimpse of a girl in the distance that resembled Meg, a sound in song, a place we sat at and memories would flood in and I would miss her again. An alienated parent never has rest; at any turn of the corner a reminder of indescribable loss may strike.

i. *Hope turns to despair; plans, goals – what was, what might have been.*

A loving parent has nothing but hope for his or her child, that they will first and foremost escape the harms and hurts of life. That they will mature to become upstanding and contributing individuals in society. That is what I hoped for my children. When Megan became a Junior Olympic swimmer, I hoped that she would be the first of our four children to be offered a scholarship so that she could attend college. I wanted her as a woman to be able to choose a career that allowed her to be completely self-reliant.

Instead, when she was taken, she was pulled from the pool forever. Now I read on Twitter that she relies on FAFSA and college loans while working at different jobs periodically. Parental Alienation destroys hopes and dreams, it replaces it with what was, what might have been.

j. *Dreams – demons of reminder in the night.*

I'm not sure if this is normal with all alienated parents, but in my case, dreams come every so often in the night. I suppose in my case it is because I had so many moments and memories with Megan, unlike many parents whose children are taken before they could rightfully have them. I have dreams of Megan, infrequent meetings with her in years ahead and do even now.

She comes briefly, sometimes when I knew her when she was little, sometimes at the age she was taken, sometimes at an age when she has grown older. They come without notice and I wake and remember. As I write them down I am struck by how vivid they are, so much so that sometimes that they seem more real than life itself:

> *I saw her at the mall. It was a surprise, unexpected. Years later. But she looked the same as when I knew her, and the times when I took her there. Sitting there with her smile, and with her laugh. As she always did, with the friends she loved.*
>
> *I approached her, and looking down at her, our eyes met. I couldn't say anything, but the tears streamed down my face. They spoke of how much I missed her, and then I turned and walked away.*
>
> *She got up, and headed towards me, and she called out, "Dad." A name of all my names I loved the most. I turned, looking at her, and said, "No one else in this lifetime, will ever love you as much as I do."*
>
> *I had a deep need to tell her, and I did, "I hope for all the best for you, that sorrow and pain don't find you, that only happiness and fulfillment, follows you in all the days of your life."*
>
> *For some unknown reason, I couldn't stay. "You have to go now," I said to her, and I turned and left. And as always, she was gone.*
>
> *And I found a place, sat, and sobbed.*

But I know I'll see her again. Because the dreams don't go away, they'll come back another day. Another visit:

> *I was staying on a farm, owned by a kind and elderly woman and her husband. It was early evening and flurries had started. The dream so vivid I thought I could reach out and catch the snowflakes. The details so real, the white blanket of clouds and its storm front foretold the coming*

snowfall, while the last rays of the sun on the horizon cut through the cold and gave some warmth.

I went into one of the buildings on the farm, an old single room with a wooden serving bar in front, and seats with small tables scattered throughout. I was standing around by the bar, talking with the owners and their sons, daughters and spouses. Out of the corner of my eye I saw Megan, sitting alone at one of the tables. I knew she was looking at me but I was afraid to look back, for fear of breaking down. She did not know I had seen her.

Suddenly, someone came in and told us we had all better leave. The storm had turned for the worst and if we did not go then, the snow would get too deep to leave. We left, and the dream did not permit me to see where we went, or let me know where Meg went.

Later in the evening, the snow storm unexpectedly stopped and we returned to the farm. I was walking down the hallway of the main house, with the rooms on my right. Approaching one room, I saw the kind and elderly woman standing within the doorway, and before being able to see in, she said to me, "Someone wants to see you."

I walked in and Megan was lying on the bed, near the foot of it, ready for sleep as she did many years ago when she waited for me to return home from work. Wrapped in a blanket, with her head on her pillow. But she wasn't 18 as I had seen her hours earlier. This time she was 4 or 5 years old. I knelt down at the foot of the bed and looked over her, as I did all those years ago. And my thoughts returned to those years before …

When I would return from working in the heat of summer or cold of winter at UPS after a 10 or 11-hour day, her mother would tell me when

> *I entered the door, "Megan is waiting for you." I would go up and there with her was Princess, her soft-pink stuffed animal. And there was Hippo, her soft-blue stuffed animal friend. I was Hippo, she was Princess. They were the "bestest" of friends. For 10 to 30 minutes a night we had parties, dinners in and out. We went to the movies with all her other stuffed friends. Gorilla was the bully. At times, Hippo had to come to the aid of Princess and her friends. Sometimes I would intentionally call Princess "Precious" to incur the reprimand, "Princess, Daddy!" from Megan. Each time would end with either a small complaint, "Just 5 more minutes?", or an "Ok" as she rolled over and close her eyes. Or I would suddenly hear the rhythmic breathing pattern of her sleep.*
>
> *These were the times the hard days at work made it all worth it. These were the moments that I placed my hand on her head as she fell asleep and whispered, pleaded, to a higher power: "Please keep her safe. Keep me safe to protect her."*
>
> *As I looked down at her in my dream, she laughed and chuckled as I saw and heard her years before. But suddenly tears welled up in my eyes. I knew, as always in these visits, that time was short.*
>
> *I had to ask the question - "Meg, did I ever do anything to you, to hurt you?" Her smile left and she nodded, slowly, but determinedly, "No." Not with a look on her face of "I don't understand the question" but rather "Why the question?"*
>
> *Unlike past visits, this time there was no goodbye.*
>
> *She was just gone.*

Like past visitations, the dream was short, fleeting. But, as always, I awoke with lasting impressions and deep sorrow, with questions unanswered and sleep that is elusive. I believe the reason for the dreams is the void between the time you knew of the child you loved and the present "not knowing." The ultimate cruelty of Parental Alienation.

k. *Each day, the question - What becomes of her?*

I can't be there when she needs me, I won't even know when she needs me. The alienators, courts and psychiatrists denied me that fundamental right as a parent. I am left wondering, worrying . . . "*As waiting the long years through, in the dust of that little chair, what has become of our Little Boy Blue, since he kissed them and put them there . . .* "

III. The Sorrow of Parental Alienation Syndrome

For the alienated parent, the sorrow of Parental Alienation is catastrophic; it affects the mind, the body and the heart. One family member once commented that I was filled with self-pity. This is another misunderstanding of Parental Alienation. The alienated doesn't weep for him or herself. The alienated parent weeps in sorrow for the tragedy he or she witnesses of seeing the ongoing abuse of their deeply loved child, and for the loss of their child, a sorrow that never leaves.

a. *Physically - Tears.*

Never did I ever think that the human body had the ability to create so many tears. In private, the sorrow runs so deep that the tears flow freely. In public, the stoic weeping – the body's ability to weep with dry tears, under a hat in a corner, down an aisle in a grocery store, or in a seat at a pub.

b. *The Mind – Memory Triggers and Ghosts.*

Memories are both a blessing and a curse to the alienated parent. Deep in the conscience lives all the memories a parent has of their child. Even if the memories could be removed, the paradox is that we would never choose to do so. Not when there are such powerful memories filled with love and joy. But the curse is the "memory triggers" that come. Triggers, places and people you encounter that unexpectedly remind you of memories of the child who is missing from your life.

The mind recalls moments of when you held them, when you reached out to help them, when they made you laugh, and most of all, when you just enjoyed the thousands of times they were beside you . . . and then it creates ghostly images of them, hoping the child is truly there, only for them to fade away. The heart then endures the harsh reality that they are no more.

c. *The Broken Heart.*

As an alienated parent, I have come to know what heartbreak truly is. I once thought that the term "broken heart" was a figure of speech, fine prose for a writer's fictional story. But I experienced the reality of a broken heart.

Each time Megan faded away, my heart heaved, shuddered, and then wept . . . uncontrolled by number, time or place.

PART IV – COURTS & COUNSELORS

Chapter 14

Our Broken Judicial System – It Isn't Just About Our Children

When Megan was first taken by her mother, the system told me the first lie. My first family law attorney explained to me that to get Megan back I would have to file for divorce. Believing that this would be the only way to get my daughter back from Texas I followed the advice of my attorney. Having no "extra" money or savings at the time, I had to borrow money from my brother Donnie to pay the attorney's fees.

My wife's family, specifically her brother-in-law Jamie, earned a huge salary from the Texas Rangers, and he also made money from licensing commission. Right out of the gate, I could not compete with their wealth. For the first year or so I questioned myself; "Surely a court will not have me pay my ex-wife's legal fees, as that only encourages other family members to get involved, which only encourages separation and divorce." I was so naïve. The family law court system only encourages such. Alimony and child-support deposited into the central system is matched dollar-for-dollar by the federal government. In essence the courts are rewarded for the funds they bring in. Do you remember my petition to modify income? The one that Judge Schoonover refused to hear? I could not for the life of me figure out why . . . until I began to educate myself in order to defend myself because I could no longer afford an attorney (or much else). Imagine my shock when I became aware of the fact that the lowering of my alimony payments meant that the courts would earn less money.

From the moment that my income changed – thanks to the DCF call – I filed the income modification order required by the courts. To this day . . . as I write this, I am still fighting. My daughter is gone . . . taken . . . and I am still fighting to have the modification heard.

In a system that is rewarded for how much income they bring through alimony and child support, is it any wonder that I was to pay well above the amount of money we lived on for over 30 years?

Florida Law states the following:

61.08 Alimony. -

(a) The standard of living established during the marriage.

(b) The duration of the marriage.

(c) The age and the physical and emotional condition of each party.

(d) The financial resources of each party, including the non-marital and the marital assets and liabilities distributed to each.

(e) The earning capacities, educational levels, vocational skills, and employability of the parties and, when applicable, the time necessary for either party to acquire sufficient education or training to enable such party to find appropriate employment.

Over a year after losing Meg, I met with a law firm through a friend that needed a new website. I bartered with them and they started proceedings to have my family law case moved from Seminole County to Broward County. While I couldn't afford to pay the $2,500 per month, I had sent my ex-wife over $7,000 in the prior year. Even so, the arrears had now risen to almost $70,000 despite the still outstanding petition to modify income, which sat there on the docket for two years.

In April of 2015, my attorneys presented a motion I had filed the year before to overturn the original divorce decree. It wasn't the petition to modify income I had expected to be heard. My attorneys stated that with the transfer of the case to Broward County, "The docket was all screwed up. All the docket items were dated the same, instead of when each was originally filed. All of the documents had the same October date of when it was transferred and they could not find the petition to modify income."

The motion was denied and the $2,000 in lifetime alimony continued to accrue. Furthermore, my attorneys found out that a hearing had been held without my knowledge in December of 2013, with regard to another of my ex-wife's contempt motions. Without being served, without a notice of hearing or without a notice of order, I was ordered to pay my ex-wife $2,000 or a warrant for my arrest would be issued and executed.

A month later there was another hearing addressing a new contempt filing made by my ex-wife – while my petition to modify income continued to sit there unaddressed. Instead of a judge, this hearing was held by a magistrate who began by asking what the case was about since "the docket was a mess" – her own words. My attorney said they were having extreme difficulty with the docket too. So much so, that he could not respond to some of the assertions because he could not even comprehend the status of the case. To make matters worse, I was informed that because I was represented, I was not allowed to speak unless I was asked a question. My ex-wife, however, being without counsel, was not bound by the same restriction; she was allowed to speak freely.

With respect to the contempt I was facing, there are two requirements in family law by which contempt can be met and denied: (1) If a petition to modify income is filed as I had done, and (2) If circumstances change. For me, there was both.

However, when the magistrate stated that she "couldn't change the original alimony order as there is no apparent petition to modify income filed," I attempted to tell her there was, to which she said simply, "Sir, I told you not to speak." With respect to the "change in circumstances," when asked why I couldn't afford to continue to pay, I informed the magistrate of my attempts to find suitable work to no avail.

Further, I testified to the magistrate that a year prior I had almost severed my right hand in a horrific accident while moving a glass table top. I was left with 60% loss of feeling making it difficult to perform my work as I used to. I presented the doctor's statement of the micro-surgery and what he informed me was a permanent disability.

Despite my responses and evidence, contempt was upheld, and the arrears of almost $100,000 now accrued. I was also informed that despite having no assets, renting a room and paying monthly for use of a vehicle, my ex-wife's "support comes first before I pay my own support, food and shelter."

The last subject to come up was the last thing I owned. My pension,

$882 per month. I was ordered to pay the only cash I had – $400 in the bank – and my future pension of $882 that I had not yet received (which would only be $632.00 after taxes.). I had no expectation of income that month, which the court was well aware of.

I was still ordered to pay $1,275. If not paid upon receipt I would be incarcerated for six months in the county jail.

Prison.

Over thirty years dedicated and committed to my wife, supporting and raising four children, and this is where it led to. All worldly assets were gone, shredded by divorce and alienation. All money spent on the family law division. Megan, my fourth child, allowed to be taken by her mother not once, but several times, and finally ordered by a court to be taken from me. The only thing left was the writ for my arrest, the last thing that could be taken: my body, my freedom.

When I received the magistrate's order, I was stunned. First, the debilitating injury to my dominant right hand was referred to as "suffering from a recent hand injury." Second, the court assertion that I had the ability to pay not only the monthly lifetime alimony of $2,000, but an additional $400 for the arrearage, $2,400 per month. Finally, that I had the ability to pay the contempt purge of $1,275 to stay out of prison.

With all of the unexplainable contents of the recent court orders, I began studying and researching both family law and contempt laws. I had no choice but to learn. I had to fight or go to prison.

The first step was to file an Exception to the Magistrate's Report. With the website completed for the law firm, I could not afford to pay them to continue on the case and so I began again pro se – representing myself. Sometimes, as the adage goes, "he who represents himself has a fool for an attorney." Unfortunately, I was like so many others involved in family courts: bled dry, left with no other choice.

Knowing how important the time frames for filing were, that missed deadlines meant my motions would be "forever lost," I immediately filed my Exception on the tenth day as allowed by law. The very next day I unexpectedly received the judge's order ratifying the magistrate's Exceptions – time had not even lapsed to allow me the proper time to respond. I filed a Motion to Vacate. Even if the lower court ruled against me, I was going to appeal. But rules had to be followed and the first was to properly set the record.

In the Motion to Vacate I quoted court rules – again I had ten days. I attached the exhibits of a parking receipt and the stamped court copy I had made sure to get when I filed my Exception. I had to, because the court docket didn't have record of my filed Exception. The Clerk of Court had not filed it.

Once again, the court came back unexpectedly fast, and by sua sponte – i.e. actions taken by a judge without prior action of either party – vacated their own order and scheduled a hearing on my Exception. Knowing that a court can hold a sua sponte hearing like this at any time, I wondered why my petition to modify income continues to sit unaddressed, even after 3 long years …

In preparing for the Exception hearing, I scrutinized court rules and Florida Family Law and registered for an online case law site called VersusLaw.com, an inexpensive, comprehensive legal research site where legal decisions and opinions can be searched to determine rulings in any state – in my case, Florida.

I also hired a court reporter to be present at the Exception hearing with the lower court. When Megan was ordered to Texas in 2013, I appealed. The appeal was denied for the simple reason that there was no "record" – meaning, I hadn't hired a court reporter so the hearing had no transcript. With my appeal and exhibits, I had done everything right, my arguments could have been completely right – except that I did not hire a court reporter. Unlike federal law where court reporters are mandatory, in state courts they are only required with magistrates, but not judges. I learned a hard lifetime lesson fighting for Megan.

Now I was faced with another choice: pay the $400 and the subsequent $882 in pension I was waiting for to stay out of jail, or pay for my right to have a court reporter at the hearing and the cost of my inalienable right to appeal. It really wasn't a choice; I wasn't going to have $1,275, not when taxes would be taken out.

There were three main issues I presented to the court with respect to the magistrate's Report and Recommendation: 1) Alimony, 2) Child Support and 3) the Purge set for contempt to avoid prison.

With respect to alimony, I abided by the law and filed the modification three years earlier. It has not only remained unheard, but the magistrate stated that it "didn't exist." While the magistrate and my attorney couldn't find one, I presented the prior Seminole Court docket that showed it. Still I was denied.

With respect to child support, there was never a relocation motion filed by my ex-wife.

With respect to the contempt charge, there are two types: criminal and civil contempt. I was being held under two types of "civil contempt." The first was that I was ordered to pay $2,000 per month in lifetime alimony which the magistrate ruled I had "wantonly and willfully refused to pay." Despite all of the evidence I produced to the contrary.

Once the magistrate ruled as such and held me in the first contempt, this led to the second civil contempt, where I was ordered to pay a "purge" amount of $1,275 or face prison. With civil contempt, there is no trial, no jury, the contemnor can simply be held up to 180 days in prison.

However, there comes a caveat: the contemnor must have what court decisions have called the "keys to his cell," i.e. the ability to release himself by paying the purge amount. If he is not able to do so, under federal law, the civil contempt becomes one of criminal contempt and the contemnor must have all rights under the law afforded to him or her: the right to counsel, the right to a jury, and the right to a fair trial.

I didn't yet have $882 in my pension check - nor would I ever after the deduction of taxes.

In my case, the contempt included my portion of the pension, the only money I had beyond the $400 in my bank account. I asked that the magistrate's recommendation be overturned, or in the alternative, the contempt become one of criminal contempt so that I could at least plead my case to a jury.

After the twenty-minute hearing the court stated, "The petitioner's objection is denied. He can work at McDonald's or do something, whether it leads to jail that remains to be seen."

As I write this book, the alimony arrearage is well over $100,000 now and within two years will grow to $150,000. In four years it will be $200,000, multiplying on itself. It will be a vicious circle, contempt, hearing, purge set, appeal again and again, one that a job at McDonald's will not cure.

Instead of paying alimony, I now hold onto what little money I can for the next hearing. I pay for the next court reporter, the next transcript.

To pay for my right to appeal the next contempt and order, and the filing fee of the next appeal. Only to do it all over again. Thousands of dollars each time.

I hold the habeas corpus in my pocket.

> A writ of habeas corpus is a judicial mandate to a prison official ordering that an inmate be brought to the court so it can be determined whether or not that person is imprisoned lawfully and whether or not he should be released from custody.

As I researched family and case law, constantly facing wall after wall despite complying with both, it became clear that it wasn't really for "the best of interests of the child;" it was about money. Tax money. States cannot accrue "annual debt" as the federal government can. States must balance their budgets every year. Family law is a trillion-dollar business and without those trillions of dollars, a vacuum will occur. It is parents, grandparents, aunts and uncles, cousins, nieces and nephews, grandchildren … and most importantly, our children that suffer under this behemoth system. And it does so ignoring one of the greatest consequences: Parental Alienation. It fuels the behemoth.

In 2005 a document was published by the *Child Support Enforcement Council* entitled, "How the System Works" with regard to the partnership between the federal government and the states, stating:

> Established in 1975 under a new part D of *The Title IV of the Social Security Act, the government -D program,* usually called the ***Title IV-D program*** *is a Federal/State partnership whose primary mission is to enforce child support obligations against non-custodial parents.*
>
> ***At the federal level the IV-D program is administered*** by the Office of Child Support Enforcement (OCSE) within the Department of Health and Human Services. It is responsible for providing regulatory oversight, as well as technical assistance to the States and territories for the effective operation of their Title IV-

D programs, in conformity with the requirements of Federal law.

The Federal government provides the major funding for the administration of the Title IV-D program, including matching funds to the States for eligible ***administrative expenditures and incentive payments*** *for program performance meeting Federal standards. The Office pays the major share of State program operating costs, provides policy guidance and technical help to enforcement agencies, conducts audits and educational programs, supports research, and shares ideas for program improvement.*

At the State level, the IV-D program is administered through a single entity designated by the State as its Title IV-D agency in accordance with an approved State Plan meeting Federal requirements. In most States and territories, the designated Title IV- D agency operates under an umbrella human services or social service agency, ***while in others it is a component of the State's department of revenue or attorney general's office***.

State IV-D programs are required to provide services to families receiving public assistance and to other families who apply for services. *The State program must attempt to locate non-custodial parents, establish paternity, establish and enforce support orders, and collect child support payments. In spite of increased Federal funding, from FY 1997-2005 the amount of uncollected child support in the national CSE program's caseload rose from $45 billion to $106 billion. Currently,*

> *less than half of all recipients of Title IV-D services ever receive the child support which they are due.*

In just eight years, by 2005, the uncollected amount of $45 billion dollars more than doubled to $106 billion dollars. I can only imagine how much this amount has risen since then, and how many mothers and fathers, as in my case, didn't simply refuse to pay, but rather, had income modification taken away, their children taken away and their families torn apart so that the state could claim further support payments – to then be matched by federal funds.

Not only matched, but the federal government pays a majority of the funding once the state systems are set up and in adherence with federal requirements. For example, in Florida law, the office of the Clerk of Court shall operate a "depository for alimony transactions, support, maintenance, and support payments; fees." The federal government, via the federal child support cost reimbursement program, will then reimburse the depository "for services provided under a cooperative agreement with the department pursuant to s. 61.1826."

It is the funding of the federal government to the "depository" of the states. Trillions are paid, billions go unpaid, not only by those who refuse to pay, but by many who are unable to. I'm in an industry that understands this process. The more "inquiries" I received in an internet department, the more I could convert to "sales." For every 100 internet inquiries, 30-40 were "unqualified" leads, they couldn't buy, but they were now in the system. The remaining 60–70 leads became "set appointments" and from there it became a scale: 50% became "shown appointments," and of those 30–40 they converted 15–20 to sales. Likewise, for each parent placed in the depository system it is a conversion process, some can pay, some refuse to, many simply cannot. The more inquiries I could get into my internet system, the more I could convert to sales. The more "wards of the state" a state can get into their "depository," the more matching funds it can acquire from the federal government.

States, as in Florida, set up "Trusts" in adherence with federal law so that federal money acquired from national taxes can in turn, pay the states. Florida has a number of "trusts" set up to receive the federal funds, most of which are to be administered by the Department of Revenue:

> **61.1811** Clerk of the Court Child Support Enforcement Collection System Trust Fund.
> **61.1812** Child Support Incentive Trust Fund.
> **61.1814** Child Support Enforcement Application and Program Revenue Trust Fund.
> **61.1816** Child Support Clearing Trust Fund.
> **61.1824** State Disbursement Unit.

The state, the law, the court and the depository, as in my case, doesn't give advice on what course to take when an emergency sets in for a father or mother ordered to pay support, especially when involved in Parental Alienation - it doesn't care. The parent is still expected to pay alimony and child support even though, despite every effort, they are quite literally unable to do so. As they scramble to act for the stability of the child they love, the "wheels of justice" turn slowly through a seemingly endless stream of motions and petitions.

When the court allowed Megan's mother to take her to Texas, it gave authority not only requiring me to continue the $2,000 per month alimony, but an additional $480 plus per month plus child support – and with no time sharing. Now almost $2,500 into the repository, another $2,500 or more from the federal government. How many parents are caught up in the system and can't pay? How many parents have been torn from their child or children? How many families, grandparents, aunts, uncles, cousins, nieces and nephews separated and torn apart by Parental Alienation because the courts won't acknowledge it, because of the numbers game, i.e. The Depository.

When I first encountered the system, I couldn't understand how the law could be on my side in statute, but not in practice. How an entire system in place to protect our rights as parents – and especially our children – was instead encouraging separation and divorce, i.e. the accrual of legal fees.

I met a father who worked two jobs seventy hours per week and still couldn't keep up his support payments. His ex-wife filed contempt charges and he was sent to prison with a contempt purge of $10,000. Of course he didn't have it. After several days and pleading with his father, his father paid $10,000 to release him. I realized later in researching the law and the "depository" that it encouraged precisely this; it is a trillion-dollar business and it matters not where the money comes from as long as it comes, never mind the devastation and destruction of families it leaves in its path.

I have also come across parents, fathers and mothers who lost all financial stability, their credit destroyed, their business licenses and driver's licenses suspended or denied as penalty over their inability to keep up with support payments, as states, including Florida, can take that away too. Life, liberty and the pursuit of happiness no longer applies to these selected "wards of the state." From income deduction to denial of professional licenses to credit reporting, the state acts as an enforcer – not in the best interests of the child, not in support of parental rights, but in pursuit of legal fees for the depository, for their slice of the pie, i.e. federal funds.

I had three law firms under family law working my case. Not one informed me - nor do they usually inform others – that under civil contempt purges, the loss of these freedoms will not occur if you can pay what little money you do have. What that means is that we have the "keys to our cell," to our licenses, at least some semblance of our ability to live with the basic necessities of life. In Florida, the Supreme Court ruled in Gregory v. Rice that:

> When a parent fails to meet a child support obligation, a trial court may hold the delinquent parent in civil contempt. **However, the trial court is authorized to do so only when the parent has the ability to pay a purge amount.** The court explained that "regardless of whether the sanction is incarceration, garnishment of wages … [or] the

> revocation of a driver's license, ...the court must provide the contemnor [i.e., the non-paying parent] with the ability to purge the contempt." If the delinquent parent has no "present ability" to pay the purge amount, then he or she cannot be held in civil contempt.

In 2005, Florida's Fourth District Court of Appeal in *Larsen v. Larsen*, 901 So.2d 327 (Fla. 4th DCA 2005), extended this line of analysis to cover suspension of the driver's license of a parent who fails to meet a child support obligation. The Larsen case explained that "[b]ecause the suspension of a driver's license constitutes a civil sanction," the trial court must first "determine that the contemnor [i.e., the non-paying parent] has the present ability to pay the purge amount."

The Larsen case explains that the statute must be read in the context of the Florida Supreme Court's Gregory v. Rice decision, that a driver's license suspension is a civil sanction requiring the court to find "a present ability to pay the purge amount in order to enter the civil sanction." *Gregory v. Rice*, 727 So.2d 251, 253-254 (Fla. 1999).

Yet parents remain imprisoned, their licenses suspended, unaware of these statues, made none the wiser by attorneys or legal advice. The depository demands the money, whether it comes from them or family members or friends, while the parent faces the scarlet letter of being a "deadbeat parent." Occasionally I hear of parents committing suicide under the weight of these burdens, and sadly am not surprised; there is no out.

Though my divorce occurred in Florida, my research is not limited to this state. There are parents losing their children to PAS every day. The failure of the American Psychological Association to recognize PAS and the unwillingness of the courts to take action to actively protect a child's right to have a loving relationship with both of their parents continues to promote the destruction of families all over the world.

One would think that the rights and well-being of the child would come first. One would think that both parents would put their child first and "sacrifice" their own wants for the needs of their child. That is what I thought and believed with all of my heart.

When all of this began, I believed in truth and the justice system. I have learned that the truth means very little when it comes to who has the best legal counsel – and a bottomless money pit from their brother-in-law. Anne manipulated the courts and her family with total disregard to what was - and is - best for our daughter Megan. The best parent didn't win; the best person didn't win. We all lost, even Anne.

If prison is to be my lot in life, I can do nothing but accept it along with the revolving door of habeas corpus. If it is limited wages that are now my lot in life, no matter the struggle to raise it, I can do nothing but accept it.

I have to accept that the court holds the tethers of my life until it is over – what I have, where I go and what I do by the shackles of lifetime alimony and alimony arrears in ignoring a petition to modify years ago. I am not "free" as many Americans are under our constitution – enjoying the full benefits of life, liberty and the pursuit of happiness.

What is hard to accept under alienation and court ordered lifetime alimony is the realty that Megan was taken, that I have been denied the God-given right as a parent to be there for my children, either in word, deed or support, because of Parental Alienation, under the suffrage of family law.

Chapter 15

The Psychiatric Community – Blinders on the Window of Alienation

"Megan doesn't understand why you don't talk to her about all of this," our second counselor, Christie, said to me in one session. "How can I?" I asked Christie. While presented as a question, it really wasn't. I knew the answer. With Parental Alienation, the threat of relocation was like a sledgehammer held over my head by my wife for over a year from the first-time Megan was taken to Texas until the divorce trial.

While most of the 20 determining points dependent for relocation of a child (or not) in Florida favored Megan's stability in Florida, the one I held most sacred was to protect her from the ongoing litigation between her Mom and me. I kept as much as I could from Megan as to my thoughts and beliefs of what her mother was doing, especially when it came to Parental Alienation. I certainly was not going to discuss the legal matters with Megan. It broke my heart just seeing what she was going through.

It was especially Florida statute 61.13 under family law that I was not going to violate:

> (r) The capacity and disposition of each parent to protect the child from the ongoing litigation as demonstrated by not discussing the litigation with the child, not sharing documents or electronic media related to the litigation with the child, and refraining from disparaging comments about the other parent to the child.

With such a question, "Megan doesn't understand why you don't talk to her about all of this," as our counselor asked, it was that question that hauntingly kept coming back to me through four counselors, especially the last one who not only seemed oblivious to, but eventually ignored that one major point - because it was that point which is closest to that of Parental Alienation.

I had never experienced Parental Alienation, let alone know what it even was in my thirty years of parenting. With that ignorance of such a syndrome, who does the alienated turn to if not the counselors and psychologists?

I explained the law to Christie and asked her, "What am I to say to Megan?" Silence was the answer. I have found that, in researching Parental Alienation on website after website and seeing forum after forum of alienated parents, the responses are all the same – each with parent after parent asking "Why? How can this be?"

The paradox was so much worse with my Parental Alienation as I responded to Christie. When Megan was first taken to Texas, Anne's brother-in-law Jamie stated to my sister that my own children were going to testify against me. Can you imagine? No abuse over the course of thirty-two years of marriage and my own children were going to testify on things never seen. The witness list was provided to my attorney, and my second daughter Erin was listed. I told Christie about the Facebook post by Erin that alleged she witnessed the abuse and that was the reason she "had to leave for Texas." As Christie listened, I went on to describe that Erin had left because she wanted to be with her cousins. When she became irresponsible and stopped paying rent, she had a falling out with both her mother and I, and cut off all communication as we informed her she would be required to pay for her own car insurance.

I told Christie that when I had to move out of the home my wife and I shared after being informed that Anne was never coming back, my sisters found hand-written notes by my wife asking Erin why she "had cut us off and why she was being so irresponsible." The letters also revealed the real reason why Erin had left. I then informed Christie of the unfathomable paradox: "Do I stay silent and fail to produce the letters and lose Meg?" Or, "Do I produce the letters and show that my own daughter committed perjury on the witness stand?" I asked, "So what do I do?" I didn't expect an answer, as my counselor's face acknowledged and reflected the anguished decision I had to make. An answer never came, and it hasn't with all the counselors I hired nor the final counselor ordered by the court.

On the second day of our divorce trial, Erin came to the courthouse and I saw her out in the hallway. During the morning session there was a break and I stepped out of the courtroom. There was Erin, with her mother's sister Jean sitting next to her, as if coaching her at a sporting event with her finger up in her face, I could just imagine the words: "You can do this!" - to my own daughter, against her own father.

Erin took the stand and testified for ten minutes, detailing alleged "abuse" she witnessed over her entire life, and why she had to "get out" and go to Texas. How Megan should be protected from me. When I took the stand, my attorney produced her mother's letters, those that proved it was all a lie. Her mother and her aunt had manipulated Erin into perjury. The court made no mention of Erin's testimony, and at that point, Megan's mother was not allowed to relocate Megan to Texas. But the damage was done, more victims strewn and laid out by the scorched earth, another consequence of Parental Alienation.

While I did my best to comply with the twenty factors to keep Megan in her stable environment, it was her mother's downfall in the months leading up to trial. Withholding communication between father and daughter, refusing cellphones to enhance communication, and her mother speaking all the time with Megan about the legal issues. I wondered why the court and counselors remained so silent on Parental Alienation, and on Anne's continued attempts at alienation until at last she succeeded.

It was eye-opening when I came across a 1997 article concerning practice parameters for child custody evaluations by the American Academy of Child and Adolescent Psychiatry. It not only recognized Parental Alienation, it recognized the need to assess the "apparent alienation" and even further, it recognized the divide within the psychiatric industry that Parental Alienation is even a "syndrome":

> **Parental Alienation**. There are times during a custody dispute when a child can become extremely hostile toward one of the parents. The child finds nothing positive in his or her relationship with the parent and prefers no contact. The evaluator must assess this apparent alienation and form a hypothesis of its origins and meaning. Sometimes, negative feelings toward one parent are catalyzed and fostered by the other

> parent; other times, they are an outgrowth of serious problems in the relationship with the rejected parent. This phenomenon, which some have called a "syndrome," has been addressed by Benedek and Scherky (1985) and by Dunne and Hedrick (1994).
> – *J. Am. Acad. Child Adolesc. Psychiatry. 36:10 Supplement, October 1997*

Despite the recognition twenty year's prior, an Academic Journal article entitled "Assessment of Family Custody Issues Using Mental Health Evaluations: Implications for Mental Health Counselors" by Samir Patel and Karyn Jones sheds light on how long the Psychiatric community has remained nearly silent on Parental Alienation Syndrome, and that even now:

> "Mental health evaluations" in the child custody dispute resolution process (also called child custody assessments or custody evaluations) evaluate family functioning to help courts make decisions on custody and visitation (Schepard, 2005, p. 187). Historically, Ph.D. psychologists have performed most of these evaluations (Ramage & Barnard, 2005; Vandenberg, 002), but as the demand for this assessment has grown in the last several years (Schepard, 2005), more professionals from a variety of disciplines and at all educational levels are now providing mental health evaluations in child custody cases (Martindale, 2007). In fact, Bow and Quinnell (2004) recently found that judges and attorneys referred 42% of cases to master's-level mental health professionals.
> Little has yet been written about the role of the mental health counselor in mental health evaluations in child custody cases.

> A thorough review of the counseling journals yielded only one article on the topic in the last 20 years (see Remley & Miranti, 1991.)

Thirty-two months after Megan was first taken and eighteen months after a court did not allow Megan's mother to take her to Texas, without warning and without notice, I was sent an email in April of 2013 by a new judge who had entered the case: a hearing was set to take place the following day. Apparently, communication between my ex-wife and the court had occurred without my knowledge; I knew not of the contents, then or even now. In that hearing the court ordered Megan, her mother and me to be interviewed by a court-ordered counseling service: Pittington Counseling Services in Lake Mary, Florida. Three interviews at thirty minutes each would likely determine the course of Megan's future and where she lived, even though she wanted to remain in Florida with her friends as she headed into her senior year of high school.

As required, I filled out the paperwork, pages of fear, concern and examples of how my ex-wife had repeatedly attempted to terminate the relationship between Megan and me. In the interview I emphatically stated the same. Afterwards, I waited for the next hearing; it came several weeks later, in May of 2013. In a ten-minute session, the court determined the final fate of father and daughter: the court ordered Megan's mother to take her to Texas.

Shockingly, when I received the court order I also received the recommendation by Pittington Counseling Services that "neither party objected that the daughter be relocated to Texas." No mention of the fears, concerns and examples that I presented to Pittington in both print and video, only a false statement that I had no objection.

In that same Academic Journal article, "Assessment of Family Custody Issues Using Mental Health Evaluations: Implications for Mental Health Counselors" by Patel and Jones, they went on to state that training and qualification with regard to Parental Alienation is sorely lacking:

> This lack of attention in the counseling literature does not reflect the reality that more master's-level practitioners are

> serving as court-appointed evaluators (Martindale, 2007; Schepard, 2005). *It may, however, be indicative of the belief that many mental health counselors lack formal training and may not be qualified to perform custody-related mental health evaluations (Martindale, 2007.)*

Thus, the questions came. Was it that Pittington Counseling Services was not qualified to perform custody-related mental health evaluations, completely ignoring one parent's concern of Parental Alienation? Or were there other motives: Did the counseling service fear referrals from the court if it did not recommend the way the court desired?

And more questions came. Why did the court call a new counseling service when there had been three other counselors who had intimate knowledge gathered through many sessions with Megan and me? Was the court afraid of the truth – that those three counselors never found a trace of abuse by me, that they would have recommended Megan stay in Florida and finish her senior year with the stability of her friends, that they would have recommended Megan not be relocated to Texas because she would lose her relationship with her father.

While all of the above is filled with questionable actions, with speculation, one fact is clear: Not one counselor acknowledged, treated or recommended based on the premise of Parental Alienation. The reality for most in the psychiatric community appears to be "out of sight, out of mind" with regard to Parental Alienation.

Until the psychiatric and counseling associations of America, including the American Counseling Association, the American Mental Health Counselors Association, the National Board for Certified Counselors, the American Psychiatric Association, the American Psychological Association, the American Psychiatric Foundation, the National Association of Psychiatric Health Systems and others recognize the abuse of Parental Alienation, it will be our children who continue to suffer the most.

Parental Alienation is a "dark secret" that the courts and many in the psychiatric community have hidden well for years. I even came across an organization called "The Leadership Council on Child Abuse &

Interpersonal Violence," and as stated on their website, they were "(formerly the Leadership Council on Mental Health, Justice, and the Media), founded in 1998 by professionals concerned with the treatment of victims of trauma, both in professional circles and by the legal system."

Note the "relationship" between the psychiatric professionals and the legal system. Incredibly, even at the time of this writing, they state with regard to Parental Alienation:

> "Some children are or become emotionally estranged from one or both parents during this process. The cause of this estrangement cannot be determined without an in-depth understanding of the family's history and dynamics. Research has shown that the issues underlying parent attachment or estrangement are complex and do not lend themselves to easy answers. *However, some child custody evaluators rely on simplistic "junk science" theories to explain the child's behavior and recommend "one size fits all" type solutions to force the child to divide their love 50-50 between their parents.*"

How is it they can sweep away the destruction, trauma and sorrow of Parental Alienation with such a phrase as "junk science" and further follow it up by ignoring the most simplistic sign of all: one parent who wishes to eliminate another parent from their children's lives? While they stated - "The cause of this estrangement cannot be determined without an in depth understanding of the family's history and dynamics," what history and in depth dynamics in my case or in many cases with respect to Parental Alienation? A father who had nothing but commitment and love for his wife and children for over thirty years, who was able to show repeated examples of how his wife tried and eventually did remove their daughter from his life. Parental Alienation attacks at any moment, with or without knowledge or concern of the past or history. And then the most horrific statement I've ever seen with regard to an article attempting to undercut Parental Alienation: "to force the child to divide their love 50-50 between their parents."

I had to catch my breath when I first read that statement. Forget that the courts recognize that both fathers and mothers have a responsibility to their children – hence a term called "child support," support that is ordered and paid by the one who can afford it, either the father or the mother. Yet here is a professional organization declaring that "love" and "50-50" shared time should not be ordered? It is no wonder that the Psychiatric community and the courts have turned a blind eye to Parental Alienation – when there are legal and psychiatric professionals who subscribe to the belief that "love" and "equal" time-sharing should not be shared among parents. In fact, the Leadership Council states that the abusive alienation of children by a parent is merely a "theory":

> Parental Alienation Syndrome (PAS) is one such theory. This unsophisticated, pseudoscientific theory explains a child's estrangement from one parent or allegations of abuse at the hands of one parent by blaming the other. The theory, developed by the late Richard A. Gardner, M.D., portrays the preferred parent (usually the mother under PAS) as an evil "alienator" who is virtually solely responsible for turning a vulnerable child against their estranged parent (usually the father under PAS).

While the Leadership Council and some of those in the psychiatric community would classify the "evil alienator" as the mother or a woman instead of recognizing men also alienate their children shows clearly how far they would go to debunk Parental Alienation.

Parental Alienation knows no gender. Fathers commit the abuse of Parental Alienation just as mothers do. Grandmothers, mothers, aunts, sisters, nieces, cousins, female friends are all victimized by Parental Alienation. My sisters, my nieces, my cousins have all been victimized by Parental Alienation, we are all alienated from Meg. How does the Leadership Council and the psychiatric community fail to recognize that millions of female victims are caught in the "friendly fire" of the assault of Parental Alienation?

For many families, what were once fun-filled holidays, seasonal family events and celebrations are now void of children, victims of Parental Alienation. In the periodic family get-togethers following my own alienation, I've seen my brother, my sisters and my cousins. I've seen their families, especially their children – around Megan's age. Each time, I've heard of their accomplishments - graduating high school, going to college, landing a new job.

But where is Meg? Little do they know. They cannot fathom both my happiness for them and my immense sadness at the same time, thinking of Meg, of my own children, no longer there. They see me smile as my cousins tell me of their daughters' and sons' accomplishments, but they don't see me leave the room and, as I've done so many times, find a private place to weep. I know they wonder why I refrain from a number of family events, but unlike the death of a child, a parent who is alienated can only wonder what was, what is, what will be. Every family gathering is a reminder of the child no longer there. It's not only a void for me, it's a void for all of our families.

Parental Alienation does not recognize gender, nor religious affiliation, color, creed, or political persuasion. In a Psychology Today article titled, "Parental Alienation and the Bystander Effect" by Edward Kruk, Ph.D, he writes:

> Harman & Biringen (in press) sampled a representative poll of adults in the United States, and found a startling rate of 13.4% of parents reporting that they have been alienated from one or more of their children by the other parent, with half of those reporting the alienation as severe. *This percentage represents approximately 10.5 million parents in the US alone who are facing what they perceive to be Parental Alienation. The sheer magnitude of Parental Alienation indicates that this is a major social problem and a social justice issue for children and families. This takes the issue out of the realm of disinterested reportage and into the realm of action.*

> And this is where the problem lies: *professional inaction in the face of abundant evidence of the large-scale and serious harms of Parental Alienation to children and parents. The real issue is the indifference of legal and mental health professionals who seem to be unaware of the existing research, deny the existence of Parental Alienation, and contribute to the harms suffered by children and parents through their inaction.* Professional incompetence in both the assessment and treatment of Parental Alienation is a serious problem, as many mental health practitioners lack knowledge and competence in working with this population (Lorandos et al, 2013; Baker & Sauber, 2012).

While all the questions left unanswered, only one hauntingly remains, that of the question quoted at the outset of this chapter: "Megan doesn't understand why you don't talk to her about all of this." Isn't that what counseling in some manner or form should have done, should have answered? Especially when a parent, and even more importantly, a child, is caught in the throes of Parental Alienation?

As I began to go through my separation and divorce, and with it the actions of alienation, the prism I looked through to see the blurred image of Parental Alienation became sharper. As it was later, reflecting on the counselor's recounting of Megan's question "Why you don't talk to her about all of this" I realized she wasn't really asking why her Dad wasn't talking about "all of this." Surely, as her mother admitted, Megan already knew everything. She also knew her Dad as he truly was, having lived through the years with him. What Megan really asking was:

> "Dad, why can't I just call or email either you or Mom when I want to?"
>
> "Dad, why can't I just be with both of you?"
>
> "Dad, will you relieve the pain of all of this for me?"

> "Dad, can you help me?"
>
> "Dad, will you be there for me when I need you?"

With the court having taken her, with the counselor's silence, my response is quietly whispered almost daily: "I'm so sorry Meg . . . I wasn't allowed to, but I tried so very hard to the very end."

When I realized the real meaning of her question, I sat and wept . . . for a very long time.

PART V – FINALITY

Chapter 16

Letters to My Children

Dear Ryan,

I am sorry for anything I ever did to hurt you. My biggest regret? Not being able to give you all that I would have liked. I did give you all that I had. When Megan was first taken, I'm sorry I didn't call you just to talk. I didn't know what to say. You had both Mom and me for your entire childhood, Meg didn't. Unfortunately, right or wrong, that was my priority, to keep her relationship with both her Mom and Dad.

If there is anything you ever recall that you believe hurt me, it is either forgotten or removed. There is no hurt, no pain, no anger of anything between us. I only remember the joy you have given me. The first child I held, the first I waited for since the moment I always wanted to be a dad. My expectations of being a dad were already high, but you raised the bar and made being your dad even better than I had dreamed of.

My heart leapt when it was announced your mother would bear a child, and I rejoiced the day you were born. I can still see the nurse's surprise when I stood there and wept as you came from the womb.

Before our isolation with each other, we became what I had hoped, not only father-son, but friends and partners, like your grandfather and I had been. I hope for the day we can resume that.

You became the son I always hoped and I am very proud of you and your accomplishments, especially becoming a servant to your community as a firefighter.

My phone will always wait for a call, but if we don't ever reconnect, I hope for nothing but the best for you.
I will love you long after my last day on earth.

Love,

Dad

Dear Colin,

I don't recall one disagreement we ever had before your Mom took Megan to Texas, before you heard from others about what came between us. Your email was our very first, yet even so, I want you to know that in my heart it is forgotten, removed. There is no hurt, no pain, no anger for anything. I only remember the joy and moments I've treasured as your father, that you have given me as my son.

I am deeply proud of you and all of your accomplishments and what you've done in the army. I have heard you are now married and have a beautiful wife. I wish you all the years of happiness together, that you grow old together.

I also heard you are now a father. I pray for the safety of your son or daughter and pray for the safety of you and your wife, to be there for your child and children.

You always have a place in my heart, but if we don't ever find our way back to each other, I want you to know that I wish only the best for you.

I will always love you, even after my last breath.

Dad

Dear Erin,

I regret that the years when you were young were

the most financially difficult for your Mom and me. I worked during the week and on many weekends to provide for Mom, you and your brothers. This affected my time with you more than with your brothers and sister.

You were the one I missed the most while you were growing up. It was difficult and it hurt me, watching my first baby girl growing up while I had to walk out the door, so many times, when I so dearly wanted to stay and be with you. The ache of missing you was palpable. It still is.

I gave you all that I had under the circumstances, but I wish with all my heart that it could have been different, that we could have had more time together.

I know you resent me for not calling you, for not contacting you when you had your disagreement with Mom and me and went to Texas. Again, you were caught in our financial distress in 2007. You were also caught in the "winds" of those outside of your Mom and me who intruded in our marriage.

The things you said after Megan was first taken to Texas, please know that they are long forgotten, removed. I only hold onto the happiness of those memories you gave me as my first baby girl.

I see you crawling with that broad smile of yours, and I wish I could go back and be there for even just a moment more. The loss runs deep, the gift of those memories of you even deeper.

I have heard you are married and have a wonderful husband. I wish you all the years of happiness together with your husband, that you grow old together as I had hoped to do with your mother.

I also heard you have a daughter and one either on the way or already born. I am sure they are beautiful. I pray for the safety of you and your children. My door is always open, but if we don't ever reconnect, know that I only hope for the best for you. I love you now and forever.

Dad

Dearest Megan,

I am so very sorry Meg.

I am so sorry you didn't have both Mom and Dad to see you through to adulthood as I did with my parents, and as Ryan, Colin and Erin did with your Mom and me.

I love you and miss you with all my heart.

You had a special place in my heart from the first moment heaven gave notice to me of you. If there is ever a true gift from heaven, you, your sister, and brothers were it. I had the great fortune, unlike with Ryan, Colin and Erin, to have spent a lot of time with you.

Your smile and laughter stole my heart from the very beginning. From the moment of conception until the last time I ever saw you, your presence was that of an angel. The day you left, heaven left too.

I felt your anxiety, I rejoiced at your healing and I celebrated your accomplishments. I don't know of any disagreement we ever had. I do know I fought for you to the bitter end, not to ever separate you from your Mom, but so you could have your Dad too.

I do recall your last words five years ago, "I love you too." I will keep them with me always.

I am sorry too that I missed your Lacrosse games, your high school graduation, getting your first job and buying your first car. I may have missed your first date.

I am so very sorry I can't be there when and if you need your Dad. I will always treasure the moments you gave me.

My door is always open, but if we don't ever find our way to be together again, I hope for nothing but the best for you, that only goodness and mercy will follow you all the days of your life, that you will love and be loved. I hope you find your true love in life, who will care and respect you.

I truly believe no one else in this lifetime can possibly love you more than I do and I will love you long after my last day on earth.

The memories you gave me are eternal - they have to be, that love I feel was, and still is, so very powerful.

I love you and miss you so very much.

Dad

Epilogue

When I was a boy and my world grew with more friends, I became aware of a void in my life by realizing that many of those my age had a grandfather to visit, who came to visit, and I'd hear my friends ask, "Grandpa, who . . . "

I didn't have a grandfather to ask about the world and our family that existed before me in a world gone by. I recall thinking many times growing up of what I missed. The times and experiences my grandfathers lived that an aged face and wrinkles gave evidence of.

I remember seeing both of my grandfather's, each just once. I was approximately six or seven and my Mom told me we had to stop at Jolly Rogers, an amusement park built in 1964 by extended family in Ocean City, Maryland, where we were to see Pop-pop, my Dad's father. It was an overcast day and all I can remember was a dark-colored car and an aged man get out, in dark clothes and hat. I watched at a distance from the back seat of our car. "That's my grandpa," I said to myself. The stop lasted just several minutes and that was the first and last time I recall having seen him – never being able to ask, "Pop-pop, what . . . "

The only time I remember seeing my Mom's father, Cecil (whom our mother was named after – Cecelia), was at nine or ten years old. He stayed one night in our house in Enfield, Connecticut and upon waking up the following morning, he had come down and I was introduced to him. Years later it occurred to me that the hello and goodbye was no different than casually meeting a stranger at a bar or pub, making some small talk and departing, never to be seen or heard from again. As he had entered and quickly left my Mom's life and my sister Bobbi's life many times, his entrance and exit with me was much quicker and a one-time event at that – never being able to ask, "Grandpa, when . . . "

To me these men were larger than life, my Dad and Mom's fathers! How I wanted to have known them and I had so many questions for them, never to be answered. I envied my friends and when I grew older and saw some of them casually ignore their own grandfathers, disregard them and take them for granted, it made me sad - many times. How much they missed when they didn't have to! For me, it was my life's most bitter disappointments and it followed me to fatherhood.

In the late summer of 1980 Anne and I told my father he would be a grandfather. It was one of the highlights of my life. My son would know his grandpa! History would not repeat itself.

But it did.

Just a month later Ryan's grandpa fell suddenly by a brain aneurism, gone before he hit the ground, and was gone. Six months later Ryan was born. A year later, Anne's father was moving a sofa with his son Greg, and while carrying it, shuddered momentarily and dropped on the ground, and was gone.

How could I have known the bitter disappointment of my youth; never knowing my grandfathers, would so suddenly be cast upon my children? The empty void I carried as a youth now as an adult filled with sadness, as periodically I would see the friends of my own children interacting with their own grandparents.

I was determined to be different than my own grandfathers, who did not want to know their grandchildren, or different than my children's grandfathers, who were denied knowing their grandchildren.

I was, even from early on as a Dad, looking forward to my own grandchildren, to enjoy, but more importantly, to answer their questions, "Grandpa, who . . . ," "Grandpa, what . . . ," and like, when with Meg, their presence would be my greatest joy in life.

Little did I know that a horrific syndrome would take a parent's hopes and dreams of a lifetime to be a grandfather and replace it with alienation and possibly prison.

I now live alone in a world of memories I hold dear to me. I have learned to keep at a distance family, friends and acquaintances who don't understand Parental Alienation, and there are many. Unless they become aware of and learn what it is, I cannot in a few moments describe to them the catastrophic events that occurred with me, seeing my youngest daughter victimized through the process and the lifetime results that affect our external families, friends and especially my children . . . and my grandchildren, who are victimized by PAS; alienated from their grandfather, a choice they did not make.

I also did not know the systems in place that do not acknowledge the syndrome and did little to stop the eventual permanent alienation. I live under a legal decision that ignored my petition to modify income while it upholds continuous contempt motions and orders simply because I can't afford to pay the monthly, lifetime alimony support that now accrues to hundreds of thousands of dollars. I save what I can for the next payment to a court reporter, the next appeal.

I live with the thought every day that instead of being able to help my children in some manner financially, I cannot support or aid one of my children if they are in need, especially when a court tells me I must provide for my ex-wife before even providing for my own expenses of food, shelter and clothing.

Should I eventually find myself under bodily arrest or have my pension taken, I have spent time in preparing a federal RICO action against those parties involved in the extortion of what I have left. Time spent in readiness of legal action instead of what I thought would be the final golden years of my life - spending time with my grandchildren.

I didn't write this book as a guide for those caught under the abuse of Parental Alienation. I am not qualified to do such a thing. That is for the courts and counselors to do, though they have done little to acknowledge – or stop – one of the most heinous of acts and abuses: the separation of a child from a parent by another parent.

I wrote this book to hopefully let those who are going through or just starting to go through this hell of Parental Alienation know what they will or may experience. To help them cope with, prepare for, and come to terms with the many emotional, psychological and physical traumas that come with Parental Alienation – and the professionals that ignore its existence.

Where does my redemption lie in the face of Parental Alienation? In recognition and acceptance. In the many times I sat alone trying to make sense of it all in the dark recesses of my mind, the actions of the alienator and enablers cannot and will not alter who I was: a loving Dad who gave all that he had to be a good parent. Just as all of those who have been alienated must believe – that they are good parents who did nothing to deserve alienation from the children they loved. It is said, "Time heals all wounds." Not with Parental Alienation. Time marches forward and the child grows; for the alienated, thoughts will always turn to their child: "Where are they? Where are they going?" It is a terrible concept, but over time the mind accepts the separation, and the alienation becomes tolerable.

My closure is also in faith, though my faith has substantially changed. Not so much in a religious or spiritual way, but in how I see others. I don't judge like I used to. Instead of judging, I have learned that there is value in each person's opinion, whether I agree with it or not. I also recognize with Parental Alienation that the alienated experiences great anger, great sadness or both. With me, the sadness ran so deep that I didn't have room for anger.

I am now convinced that while peace has been elusive, eventually the love and memory of my children will be all that remains. It becomes more focused every day, not replacing, but healing to some degree the deep sorrow of Parental Alienation.

Along with the freedom I experienced, I also finally carved out a social side for myself, a time for connection and reflection. I enjoy happy hours, sometimes at home, sometimes at a local pub. Everyone should have that for themselves, time and space for relaxation and reflection. I didn't for over thirty years. That time I lived for my wife and children.

Sad? Maybe. Do I regret what I sacrificed for during all of those years? No. I did it all for love. I wouldn't exchange one moment, one memory to take away the sorrow and pain. I would do it all over again even knowing the ending.

I came to recognize that I was as spiritual as my wife or my wife's family who condemned me. I was like my Dad; he didn't have to go to church every day, or even every week. He showed me what true spirituality was treating - others as you want to be treated. He did that with our Mom as a husband, he did that with my brother and sisters and me as a Dad. The home he and my Mom built for us was our altar, the yard was our congregation; it was a priceless childhood, together my Dad and Mom gave me a priceless gift.

Looking back, I also came to recognize that I did the same with my own wife and each one of our children as my parents had done for me. I worked for my children, sacrificed for them, taught them, watched over them, played with them, and supported them. The home I built with my children's mother was similar to that which my own Dad and Mom had built.

I sat many nights alone at the corner pub trying to make sense of it all, of my spirituality, of my existence that was shaken to the core. The harsh reality after 32 years with my wife: the alienator's abandonment, false accusations, the taking and use of our own child to seek revenge for crimes I committed in her mind, actions that to her along with her enablers justified the alienation of our child from me. Add to that the religious environment of the alienator and her enablers' judgment that ignored one of the most sacred of all scriptures: "Revenge is mine sayeth the Lord."

I also realized in those moments alone that Parental Alienation wasn't about religion, it wasn't about gender, social standing, ethnicity - it was about abuse. The abuse of mental violence against the other parent, and against a child who is taught to hate, dishonor and disrespect one of their own parents.

It took a long time to learn that the small seeds of faith and hope still exist within me, that they somehow survived the flames of Parental Alienation. The scripture and Zechariah are true – "And I will refine them as one refines silver, and test them as gold is tested." I do believe those that come out of Parental Alienation, though hurt and injured, nonetheless become extremely strong individuals. They don't give up, the small seed of faith forever hopes that their child will one day call upon them.

But where is the finality, the closure, the resolution for the children? For all of their remaining years when a dad or mom is void from their life? A child who will live years beyond those of their parents, who cannot find psychological or mental healing from Parental Alienation?

I now accept that I can't see, hear, or touch my children. I may never do so again in this lifetime. Events and moments Megan has since experienced are forever gone, never for me to have seen, never to be able to laugh with her, enjoy with her, cry for her in what came after. I ask myself many times, "*Where are you Meg? What are you doing? Are you safe?*" The questioning will end when my life is over.

But she will live on, and what questions will she ask herself through all the years of her remaining life? "*What happened to you Dad?*" Or, "*I can hardly remember, but what was it like with you Dad?*" Perhaps, though maybe not, the power of Parental Alienation was so acute she won't miss her dad, even as I miss mine almost forty years later.

I certainly expect those who take a daughter away from a father, a son from a mother, a child from a parent, the enablers as much as the alienator, will be responsible for her or him the rest of their life. When a parent is unnaturally alienated in vengeance from their child, the alienated parent's natural rights and responsibilities have been usurped. Who then becomes responsible for that child when heaven calls and requires an answer?

In my own small way I say to myself, "Heaven will sort this all out."

With Megan, my faith also came in one of those dreams I had:

> *It was there in heaven where we met again, having not seen each other for the rest of our earthly lives. There in a quiet corner, under the shade of an old Oak tree.*
>
> *We sat and talked, laughed, and cried. I asked her about what occurred in her life, her husband, her children, her grandchildren. Meg smiled with joy telling me of these things so close to her. I smiled back, picturing the moments.*
>
> *I held her hand and recalled the countless wonderful moments I had with her, how her laughter and giggles were the greatest sounds I'd ever heard and how I had missed her so much.*
>
> *And as we had done that one special night in our earthly life when she was fourteen years old in St. Augustine, Florida, as the apple of her Dad's eye – we talked and laughed, and talked some more . . . with more laughter, the kind that comes from down deep, that said, "I don't want to be anywhere else, with anyone else, and simply your presence is the joy of my life . . . "*

I long for that day.

Reference

Wikipedia's definition of Parental Alienation:

> *"Parental Alienation is the process, and the result, of the* psychological manipulation *of a child into showing unwarranted fear, disrespect or hostility towards a parent and/or other family members."*
>
> - Wikipedia.org, Parental Alienation

Online Links:

Social Media - Facebook is currently the fastest growing source of PAS information, resources and exposure on the worldwide web. New social groups and pages of the symptom are continually created. In these social pages are real-life experiences of PAS and with most of the posted threads, the symptoms of PAS are easy to recognize, as they are continually repeated.

With the evidence of such heartbreak of story after story, it becomes very difficult to understand how many, and for how long in the psychological community and legal system have turned a blind eye while victims and martyrs are telling their stories every day. With the denial of PAS, the massive worldwide number of victims have found their outlet, and these social groups and pages are growing by leaps and bounds.

Websites – There are a number of websites growing that have been created and maintained by some in the psychological profession that acknowledge Parental Alienation as a syndrome and address the trauma and destruction it causes for parents and more importantly, the child for a lifetime.

For a full list of PAS Social Media pages and Websites regarding PAS please visit our website. This list is updated periodically:

http://www.throughthepainedglass.com

If you are a victim or have a family member suffering the consequences of PAS, please write your federal and state officials and ask them to address Parental Alienation Syndrome - the courts need to recognize PAS.

https://www.usa.gov/state-governor

http://www.consumer-action.org/action

Your voice is needed. Your voice counts. To make change parents and family members victimized by Parental Alienation Syndrome must take action as a group. The APA needs to recognize PAS. I urge you to write them. There is power in numbers and experiences shared:

American Psychological Association
750 First Street, NE
Washington, DC 20002-4242

"Little Boy Blue"

The little toy dog is covered with dust,
But sturdy and stanch he stands.
And the little toy soldier is red with rust,
And his musket moulds in his hands.

Time was when the little toy dog was new,
And the soldier was passing fair.
And that was the time when our Little Boy Blue,
Kissed them and put them there.

"Now, don't you go till I come," he said,
"And don't you make any noise!"
So, toddling off to his trundle-bed,
He dreamt of the pretty toys.

And, as he was dreaming, an angel song,
Awakened our Little Boy Blue.
Oh! the years are many, the years are long,
But the little toy friends are true!

Ay, faithful to Little Boy Blue they stand,
Each in the same old place.
Awaiting the touch of a little hand;
The smile of a little face.

And they wonder, as waiting the long years through,
In the dust of that little chair;
What has become of our Little Boy Blue,
Since he kissed them and put them there . . .

– Author, Eugene Field

Made in United States
Orlando, FL
05 November 2026

90200311R10138